THE
RED
THREAD

My Fortunate Life in Telecommunications

H. Brian Thompson

ISBN-10: 0615783228
ISBN-13: 9780615783222

Published by Cosey Point Press, Easton, Maryland

Cover Art: Barry Winter, Easton, MD

Library of Congress Cataloging-in-Publication Data:
The Red Thread: My Fortunate Life in Telecommunications / H. Brian Thompson

Includes Index

1. H. Brian Thompson 2. Telecommunications history 3. Business autobiography

Dedication

For my wife Mary Ann and
my children Christi and Brandon.

Contents

Foreword

Ifirst met Brian Thompson in the mid-1990s at an auto race-track. Brian's company at the time had discovered the value of sponsoring a race team as a way to build relationships, establish the company's brand and drive business growth. We quickly formed a bond and friendship that continues to grow.

I have always been impressed with Brian's straightforward, no-nonsense manner of approaching business decisions and strategies. Identifying objectives and determining the best way to reach them is what makes him tick. He is honest and ethical and expects those around him to operate in the same way.

Brian and I share the fundamental belief that it's the collective effort of all the people within an organization – its human capital – that is a company's most valuable asset. One of the most difficult challenges any business leader faces is finding those people who are oriented to do the right thing, get the job done correctly and who enjoy solving problems. Brian believes in the importance of open and direct communication with the people in an organization, empowering managers to take chances and make decisions, and continually working to eliminate layers of bureaucracy.

Through the years and through our conversations, I have learned about Brian in his early years and his life journey to date. It has been fun to fill in some of the blanks by reading this book. I think you as a reader will enjoy the story of his challenges and successes along the way.

Roger S. Penske
Chairman,
Penske Corporation

Preface

I didn't write this book out of ego.

I wrote it for two main reasons. First, I want to offer some advice to other leaders, especially younger ones, so they can profit from my experiences both good and bad. All of us wish we could go back and do things differently - knowing what we know now. That's never possible, but perhaps others can benefit from watching how my business career has unfolded. I've made some good decisions and some that were less so. I learned from all of them, and I believe that others can too.

Second, I wrote this book for personal reasons. It is for my grandchildren so when they come of age they can understand who their grandfather was, why he did what he did, and what was important to him as far as running companies, working with others and the importance of strong ethics. It's an opportunity for me to pass along family traditions of hard work, building things that last, never cutting corners and conducting yourself in a way that brings honor to your colleagues, family and friends. So, this book is specifically for Mackenzie, Baxter, Montgomery ("Gummy"), Olivia, Ava and Isabella and a new grandson on his way. I hope they will one day read, digest and treasure it.

I also want to share my thoughts about the current state of companies and their leaders. Much of what I see energizes me, especially the advances in technology and telecommunications that produce more efficient and profitable companies. On the other hand, I see too many people start companies with the sole intention of cashing out. To me, this is not a worthy goal. Although financial rewards are certainly welcomed and enjoyed, the real importance of building companies is not only to offer financial benefits to large shareholders, but to employees, communities and the world at large.

No person is successful on his or her own, and I have many people to thank. I can't list them all here, yet most know who they are. Clearly at the top of the list, it is most important to mention my wife of 49 years, Mary Ann, and my children, Christi and Brandon, for putting up with and graciously supporting and helping to shape and mold my career at all levels. I have to mention also, those, who as mentors and friends, had a great influence on my development, my thinking, and my business success but didn't live to see it. Indeed, I truly miss them and their wisdom - Bill McGowan, David Williams, the unique Michael Bader, and my long-time friend Phil Cunningham. I am also indebted to those on the public boards on which I currently serve: Axcelis Technologies, Inc., GTT, Pendrell Corporation, Penske Automotive Group, Sonus Networks, Inc., and to the almost 40 boards, public, private, educational and others on which I have previously served. I appreciate that they have accepted my sometimes outspoken opinions and helped me to become a better board member.

I would be remiss if I did not underscore the influence of my parents and my two sisters Sheila and Alice who played early roles in my life as I evolved my sense of right and wrong and my lifelong sense of values (and humor). Finally, I would like to mention Trish Hunter who joined me during my LCI days and has been a faithful and immeasurably helpful executive assistant all of this time.

And I acknowledge the input and involvement of Larry Kahaner who drafted, redrafted and edited my ramblings to create what we hope is a readable and emotive book. I also thank our longtime friend and *mensch* Bill Stern who prodded us enough to make this happen. While they were both integral to the process, I take full responsibility for the accuracy and timing of events that they helped me recall and document.

As you read this book you will see what I like to call the *red thread*, the character traits and behaviors that have followed me through my life, ran through events, and helped make me successful.

I didn't always realize they were playing a role at the time as these traits are often easier to spot while looking backward instead of during an ongoing period. We all have our red threads that define who we are and why we act the way we do. They are our touchstones; they keep us grounded. For me, the red thread has been composed of the following strands: a sense of balance, strong ethics, loyalty, trust, self-discipline, risk taking, helping people (and allowing them to help me) and taking a long view. These have been the foundations of my success. I hope this book will help you understand your own red thread.

H.B.T. – February 2013

Prologue

Turning around LiTel Communications was going to be one of my most difficult challenges. LiTel was an opportunity to run a business the way I wanted it to be run, to use all I'd learned working for nine years at the management consultant firm of McKinsey & Company and, later, nine years at MCI, where I helped Bill McGowan and his team change the face of global telecommunications. There were other companies and jobs along the way, of course, some where I had been successful and some less so. In each case, though, as I look back at the 'red thread' that ran through them all, it was clear that what I had learned and experienced along the way - both good and bad - would be put to use here.

LiTel Communications was a long distance company established in Milwaukee in 1983 and later based in Columbus, Ohio, to take advantage of the competitive telephone industry that grew after the breakup of AT&T. LiTel was in financial distress in 1991, and I was brought in to turn the company around. I didn't know if it was possible, but I was going to give it my best shot. The company had done well for a while until competition increased in the late 1980s. It was refinanced by Drexel Burnham in 1989 but by 1991 the largest investor - investment firm Warburg Pincus - believed that CEO Lawrence McLernon and other top executives had failed to properly plan and execute acquisitions as well as implement their basic operating plans. Warburg Pincus officials also believed that the company had neglected the residential market and had gone too far afield with unrelated technologies like video teleconferencing, an expensive experiment that had little short-term possibility of success because it was an unproven technology.

Quite simply, LiTel was hemorrhaging money.

I arrived on Monday, July 5th, just after the three-day holiday, and even though McLernon was gone - I insisted that he leave before I arrived - his assistant stayed. I was glad of that because I'd have some continuity and she could keep me informed about what was going on in the company. The chief financial officer was there, too, as were many other executives. I called them all together and said, 'Some of you are going to stay here; some of you will be leaving. We have to make some significant changes.'

I asked them to gather as many people who could fit into the cafeteria - around 120 to 130 - that afternoon. I introduced myself, told them that I was from Washington, and that I was there to help them. It's an old political joke about how 'helpful' people from the government can be. It fell flat, but I moved ahead.

I decided that the best approach was to be frank and straight-forward. I said, 'This company is in terrible shape. Financially, it's a disaster from the investors' point of view. It's not meeting its objectives in sales. It's not meeting its objectives in getting new customers. It's not meeting its fundamental expectations. The company has hired many people in the last six months, and many of you in the room are new. You may not know it – although I suspect that most of you do – but you haven't been told the whole truth about what's going on. The previous leaders of the company apparently weren't upfront with you about the precarious state of the company.'

In my calmest voice I said: 'I want you to know that I'm here to try to help save this company. Hopefully we can, but I can't promise anything. I don't know much about the situation right now, although I do know the business and the industry reasonably well.'

I had brought Tom Wynne with me to the company and introduced him. Tom - whom I had picked to be my regional sales VP at MCI - brought Marshall Hanno with him to LiTel as well. I knew and trusted Tom and he knew and trusted Marshall who also had worked for Tom at MCI while they were in Chicago. I wanted everyone to know who these people were and that I had confidence in their abilities.

I continued addressing the group. 'We're going to start to understand what's going on, and we'll need your help. In the next three to four weeks as many as twenty-five percent of you will probably be let go.' I took a deep breath and continued: 'The company is so far out in front of its headlights in terms of its costs that the only way we can think about saving it is to reduce the head count.

'And let me be clear that these cuts are not because you have not tried to do your best. A lot of you came here because you thought this was going to be a great job, a great opportunity, and you're doing your damnedest. The problem is that management apparently didn't understand their part of the business. And for that I apologize. It's unfortunate. But I'm going to need help over the next couple of weeks to identify how we can trim the fat and cut the budget so that we can save the company. Our objective is to save it and then grow.'

I pressed on.

'For those of you who are going to end up getting pink slips, I'm sorry. We will be as quick as possible to make these decisions and it won't be because of anything you did. It's because the company needs to make changes. And although you probably don't want to think about it now, if you leave, and if we save the company, you will have priority among any new hires. Of course, we would understand if you didn't want to come back.

'Some in management have not been honest with you, but I promise that we will always try to be honest and straightforward. We *will* communicate with you.'

I explained exactly where the company stood financially, as well as its problems, and that it hadn't been able to make its debt payments that had come due the previous month. I was straightforward and said that we had only two choices: layoffs or bankruptcy.

I asked if there were any questions. There was silence at first. I think they were stunned by what they'd heard. But the questions came, and we answered as many as we could. Then I said, 'Well that's it. Let's get back to work.'

To my surprise, the group stood and applauded. I was completely taken aback by their response.

It was one of the most emotional meetings I'd ever conducted. It seemed to be the first time that anybody from management was upfront with the employees. Apparently, nobody had the sense of management responsibility or the nerve to tell them what really was going on. I will never forget that.

Everyone at the company had to understand that there was a new wind blowing through and there would be a different way of conducting business as we changed from LiTel to Lightwave Communications, Inc. or LCI and then LCI International.

As we moved forward, I kept in mind the most important lessons I had learned about running companies. It was management's job to make sure that all employees grasped the basic, simple facts about the company, and that they understood the company's situation. It was up to management to communicate in an honest, straightforward and ethical manner with employees.

This is the essence of leadership; it's what separates *managers* from *leaders*.

Chapter 1

"Here Comes Brian Again. What's He Selling This Time?"

We are all products of our upbringing, influenced and helped by our families, our neighborhoods, our teachers, friends, and, later in life, our business colleagues. As I considered who were pivotal in helping me succeed, I know that my parents played an early and formative role.

My mother's side was from Slovakia, which at that time was considered Austria-Hungary. They immigrated to the coal mine region in southwestern Pennsylvania where she was born in the town of Lisnering, grew up in Smock and went to high school in Uniontown. In that area, towns often were named for the nearest coal mine.

My father Hugh came from a poor family from a little town called Lurgan, in Northern Ireland, which had been a hotbed of Irish conflict. Lurgan was dominated by the Loyalists and my father was Irish to his core. Lurgan was dominated by the Protestants, and my father was Catholic. So he started out with two strikes against him.

His house at 11 Kilmain Street was about 12 feet wide with three rooms to accommodate 11 people. There was an outhouse in the back. When he was around five, my father and his older brothers would meet their father at the pub on Friday afternoon to get his paycheck and take it to their mother. He made his living as a common laborer. She would take some of the money to get his suit out of the pawn shop so that he could wear it to church on Sunday. On Monday, the suit returned to the pawn shop so they could eat for the week.

When my Dad was seven - that was in 1909 - he developed a horrible lung infection. Doctors didn't know what to do, and he spent the next nine months in the hospital. During that time, his doctors cut into his side with a saw, removed several ribs, and put in a drain to keep his lung from filling with fluid. From then on, he was in poor health and had to leave school because he had fallen so far behind. During times when his health was better, albeit barely, he worked in the potato fields.

Landowners treated workers almost akin to slave labor. They paid them poorly, worked them hard and for long hours. He was only nine years old at the time, but I'm convinced that his early experiences working in the potato fields spurred his interest in the importance of labor unions later in his working life.

Even with one damaged lung, he began smoking at age ten, a habit that he held his entire life. He fell into a rough crowd and by the time he reached 14 or so, the English-Irish home - rule conflict was heating up ignited by the Easter Rising that year. Compared to his older brother Jimmy, he was still pretty young, but Jimmy, along with his friends and cousins, were becoming involved in the fight for Irish independence. His younger brothers, Jerry and Tommy, were too young be part of the uprising.

As rioting and civil unrest grew, my father's brother became even more drawn to the cause and with several friends joined Frank Aiken who headed the IRA in support of the anti-treaty rebels. The situation became more and more explosive as civil war enveloped much of Ireland and the "pro-treaty" authorities in the Republic arrested the "anti's" in wholesale fashion. Frank Aiken and many of his followers, including Jimmy, were arrested and put in jail in Dundalk on July 16, 1922, not far from Lurgan. My grandmother didn't want my father or his brother involved in the growing violence, but when she heard of Jimmy's arrest and got word that there was a group hoping to free them, she sent my father to retrieve his brother's body if anything were to happen to him or his compatriots during the attempted escape. As the family story goes, one Padraig Quinn dynamited a hole in the Dundalk jail wall and freed Aiken and 104 other prisoners including Jimmy. Somehow my father found Jimmy there and they managed to find their way back to Lurgan. Fortunately, there were no bodies to bring home.

The violence was not only growing in intensity but spreading, until finally, in 1925, my father and his three brothers felt they had to leave Lurgan. The way my father described the situation, things had gotten too hot for them and their group. Two of their friends were arrested and incarcerated in a jail ship in Belfast Harbor for being activists. So, my father and his brothers left for America when my father was 23 years old.

Their objective was to reach Detroit, because they thought they could secure jobs in the booming auto industry. Like many immigrants from Ireland, they arrived first in Canada and had to figure out a way to cross the border from Windsor, Ontario to Detroit, even though they didn't have the proper papers. They came up with a clever scheme. They borrowed a car, some golf clothes and clubs and when they presented themselves at the border as weekend golfers, they were waved through. Despite the fact that they were illegal aliens, they managed to land jobs in the car factories. Jimmy became a painter, Jerry was a mechanic, and my dad and his kid brother Tommy both worked in the trim lines.

They were all working, making money, and having a great time. In 1926, my father and Jerry bought a car and took off to see the country. It was a working class road trip. They drove to the top of Pike's Peak. They visited San Francisco and lived with a family. They traveled through Southern California, and my dad dealt cards in some gambling joint in Tijuana. They drove to Florida and worked in Hialeah building the famous horse track. After the trip, they returned to Detroit and continued working in the auto factories.

Hugh Thompson (right) and his younger brother Gerald toured the United States in 1926. They stopped in Florida where they helped to build race tracks.
Author's collection.

Then, in 1929, just before the Wall Street Crash, my dad got lucky and won $3,000 in a baseball pool, which was a tremendous amount of money for the time. And what did he do with it? He did what every good Irish young man would have done. He returned to Ireland to show everybody how rich he had become in America. He stayed there for about six months and by the time he came back to Detroit - this time my father entered the country legally - the bottom had fallen out of the economy. He and his brothers were all out of work.

By 1932, after working many different jobs for various organizations, my father got a job with the Murray Body Corporation, which later became part of Chrysler. Around this time, my dad had met my mother Margaret, but marriage was out of the question because he wasn't making enough money, so he moonlighted as a magician, mainly performing card tricks. He called himself the *Great Koran* thinking that he could piggyback on the name of the great book of the Muslim faith, which was still mysterious and foreign sounding to most Americans. They married in 1933

4

and on their marriage license he entered his occupation as 'magician.'

My dad's passion for labor organizing began after he received in January 1933 a paycheck for 13 cents. At the time, he was being paid on piecework and there was very little work. He went to his boss and said, "This just doesn't work. I've met a woman whom I want to marry. I want to start a family, and 13 cents isn't going to do it. You've got to do something or else."

His boss responded: "Or else what?"

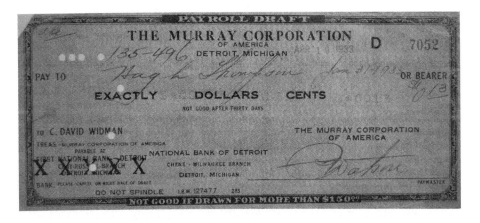

Hugh Thompson's passion for labor organizing began in January 1933 after he received a paycheck for 13 cents, and was outraged by his employer's indifference at the low amount. *Author's collection.*

My father was outraged by the unfairness of the situation, and when he came home that night he and several friends got together. They all had similar situations at work and decided that night to organize their fellow autoworkers. My father's brothers were not involved in the organizing effort as they had volunteered to be deported and had gone to England.

Being a labor organizer was not an easy or safe activity. Companies hired goons to intimidate, injure and even kill organizers. My father's offices were blown up on several occasions. One time my father was in Anderson, Indiana, with a friend to organize a plant. My mother and sister were with him. They learned that the local sheriff was planning to lynch my father, but the lawman mistook a friend, 'Pop' Kramer, for him and started beating him. The sheriff and his deputies stopped when they realized that they had the wrong man. My father had already slipped out of town with my sister and mother. If he had stayed, he probably would have been hanged.

I often think about why my father wanted to organize workers in spite of the danger to him and our family. I think it had to do with a basic sense of justice – what was right – that went back to his early experiences in the potato fields of Ireland. The second reason was the Irish culture. There is a fundamental cultural trait of trying to set things straight. He had a burning desire to make sure that people were taken care of rather than being abused. He saw that in the auto business. He had a strong ethical stance about helping people get what they deserved. He felt somewhere between outrage and indignation about how auto workers were treated.

When my father and his friends began to organize workers, they got backing from many labor leaders, including John L. Lewis who was head of the United Mine Workers at the time. The Mine Workers and the American Federation of Labor (AFL) were the only organizations fighting for the interests of labor in the country, and the Mine Workers were specific to that industry, whereas the AFL focused on the trades.

The Committee of Industrial Organization (CIO) came along in 1935 and was a federation of unions that had begun to organize workers in industrial sectors. The United Automobile Workers was part of that group, and my father was asked many times to be part of the headquarters staff in Washington. He resisted that because he wanted to be out in the field, organizing workers. It's what he loved to do, and he didn't want to be relegated to an office.

He was such a successful organizer that they made him regional director of the CIO for the western region of New York state. My mother, father and two sisters moved from Detroit to Buffalo in 1938, from where he also organized auto workers in

Canada. There, he was instrumental in establishing the Canadian Auto Workers.

Hugh Thompson received union card No. 1 of the United Automobile Workers and, being the first member, he had to sign it himself.
Author's collection.

At this point, my father was feeling confident in his job, so he, my mother and two sisters took a trip to Ireland to visit family. He and my mother went to the Armagh Cathedral in County Armagh, the final resting place of the first king of Ireland, Brian Boru. It was here that my mother told my father that if she were ever to have a son, he would be called Brian.

I was born in 1939 when my dad was on the road, as he often was, organizing workers. He was away on March 24th when my mother went into labor with me. One of the men who worked for my father drove my mother to the hospital where she gave birth. True to my mother's pronouncement at Armagh Cathedral, I was named Hugh Brian Thompson, and I've always gone by Brian.

I grew up in Kenmore, just outside of Buffalo, which was also known as *Buffalo's First Suburb.*

Even though my father was out of town a great deal, he always made sure that he took care of us. I don't think he ever made more than $12,000 in any year, but it didn't matter; he and my mother were frugal. He also did something else with his money that was unique for a union organizer. These were difficult times, and the country hadn't yet come out of the Depression. Nevertheless, when I came along they decided to buy a house in Kenmore because they had outgrown the apartment they were living in. When my parents found a house they liked and saw that there was another house on the street that was up for sale - and they kept lowering the price because the contractor was running out of money - my dad speculated and bought both houses. They turned out to be profitable deals for our family.

I had a great childhood, and did well in school. I remember skipping first grade, which was fine except that I was always the youngest in my class, and I struggled with fitting in. I had a couple of friends, and we'd play in the neighborhood and come home when the street lights went on.

I always wanted to make my own money and became creative at starting little businesses. I would go around on Saturdays with my friend Bobby Getty to collect newspapers. We'd gather them from two or three streets around, and then throw them in the back of my father's car. He'd take us to the junk dealer, where we'd get one dollar for a hundred pounds of paper. I also sold candy. I'd make potholders and hustle them around the neighborhood. The neighbors would say, "Here comes Brian again. What's he selling this time?"

When it came time to raise money for troops during World War II, we held scrap drives, sold bonds and held benefit parties in our neighborhood. We knew everyone who lived around us on St. John's Avenue. It was a true middle class existence.

I was a frugal boy and opened a bank account at school. You gave the teacher your quarters and dollars, and she would stamp your book. I felt pretty cocky about having a bank account.

In many ways, my father was a stereotypical Irishman of the time. He came first at the dinner table, and my mother waited on him. The dinner had to be cooked just right although he actually cooked sometimes, too. He never had any formal education, but he taught himself to read and write. He got into the habit of challenging us kids so he could show that he was smart. He could be very argumentative, so you had to prove everything you said. I guess it was part of the way in which he learned, and therefore he wanted to make sure that we were learning. If you said something was black, he'd say, "No, it's white," just to create an argument. Then we'd have to go through a long discussion.

He had a constant intellectual curiosity about goings-on around him, which is a trait that I picked up. It became really important to me as I grew older, and it may be one of the most helpful parts of my personality, especially in my business life.

Along with that curiosity came constant questioning about the right thing to do, both emotionally and intellectually. When I took on leadership positions later on, I would always ask myself: 'Why am I doing this?' To my father, and to me, it was important to create opportunities for people. I relish creating opportunities for people who never thought they had them. To see people succeed beyond their expectations is one of the greatest joys. You're creating a sense of self-worth in people that is extremely valuable. My father wasn't interested in putting money in a blind man's cup but about helping someone get a job or making someone's job safer or fairer.

Between ninth and tenth grade, my family moved to Boston where my father became head of the New England region for the CIO. That only lasted about a year because later in 1955 the AFL and CIO merged after a long estrangement, and he was chosen to head the merged organization in Boston.

My dad continued to bring me to events so that I could see what he did for a living. Around 1953, he and his union had to grapple with the issue of the St. Lawrence Seaway, something that had been argued over since the 1940s. Through a series of locks and channels, the Seaway would allow ocean-going vessels to travel from the Atlantic Ocean to the Great Lakes as far as Lake Superior. It would be a boon for the Great Lakes' area, but the project was opposed by lobbyists for the railroads and some Port Authorities who believed it would hurt their businesses.

Hugh and Margaret Thompson met with President John F. Kennedy in the Oval Office. They were personal friends and supporters of the president; October 24, 1961.
Author's collection.

He understood the issue very well because of the time we'd spent living in Buffalo. In fact, my dad was part of a group of people who were intensely interested in promoting the city and they helped introduce the first Seaway bill in Congress, but they weren't able to get a law passed authorizing its construction.

I remember going to New York and Washington, DC with my dad. The CIO office building was behind Blair House on Lafayette Park, directly in front of the White House. It was a gray, three-floor building. My dad took me to meet the head of the CIO, a steelworker named Phil Murray. Allan Haywood was the vice-president of the CIO at the time, and they were both pretty impressive guys for a kid who was 11 years old. Over the next few years, my dad would take me to union dinners and meetings when I wasn't in school.

On one particular night in 1955 he took me to a dinner in Portland, Maine. It was a fundraising dinner, although I didn't fully understand exactly how it all worked.

When I entered the dining room, I was the only kid. There were probably 12 people altogether at the table. It was a fundraiser for a young man who was going to run for governor of Maine. He was trying to get money from the unions and from the Kennedys.

The man who held the purse strings for the Kennedy family at the time was Francis X. O'Brien, who was also a judge. This bow tie-wearing candidate from Maine presented his budget in excruciating detail, and it was something like $14,326, not simply $14,000. He enumerated what everything would cost down to the penny, even the water and pitchers on the hotel tables. He even said how much it would cost him to buy gas so he could campaign out of his station wagon. O'Brien gave him some money, and my dad gave him some money, and he was able to continue his campaign. Had he not received that funding, he would have dropped out. As a Democrat, he was running against the odds because Maine was a Republican stronghold, but he still ended up getting the gubernatorial nod. Then he ran for Senate. His name was Ed Muskie.

It was pretty heady stuff for a kid of 14 or 15, and I didn't understand all of it. I knew that politics was a good thing because it made people discuss issues - that's what we did in our house - and come to a resolution.

By the mid-50s the Seaway issue reached a fever pitch because of power shifts in Congress. Everett Dirksen, an influential senator from Illinois, and other Midwest lawmakers were trying to bring Atlantic Ocean access to the Great Lakes.

In Boston, lobbyists were telling newly-elected Massachusetts Senator John F. Kennedy to vote against the Seaway because it would take away traffic from Boston ports. However, Kennedy was in favor of it because he felt that it actually would bring more traffic to Boston from ports in Savannah and Philadelphia. Kennedy was slated to debate James Michael Curley, who was the former mayor of Boston, former governor of Massachusetts and a political icon.

They were going to debate the Seaway at the Knights of Columbus Hall in South Boston.

Kennedy's staff learned that my dad knew about the Seaway issue. They also felt that the senator didn't understand it in the detail that my dad did, and that it would be political suicide to debate Curley. Curley was a career politician who was fast on his feet and a strong and experienced debater. They asked if my father would take Kennedy's place.

My father agreed. I went to the Hall and watched my father debate Curley. The experience was an eye-opener for me. My father held his own. He stood up to Curley and saved face for Kennedy. Kennedy knew it, and from then on John Kennedy and my father became the best of friends.

As for the Seaway, Congress finally passed legislation for its construction, and it opened in 1959.

We had been living in Milton, Massachusetts for several years. It was a fairly tight, well-to-do town, and I attended Milton High School. In order to afford our new house, we sold the house in Kenmore and also a summer cottage that my father had purchased about 10 years earlier on Lake Chautauqua in Western New York. One of my father's friends had rented a place there and after visiting him we bought a place of our own. My uncle - my mother's brother - was a skilled handyman, and he was living with us at the time. He had taken this little cottage and turned it into a pleasant place for us to stay during the summers.

All of our money went to buy the house in Milton. It cost $20,000, a lot in those days, but it was where my father wanted to live. While in high school, I spent a lot of time studying chemistry, physics and other hard sciences, but I also was a bit of an athlete. I was captain of the tennis team, and I played baseball, football, hockey and basketball in the church league. In this regard, I was not like my dad. I was physical. I took up skiing in my senior year. I had access to a car because my dad gave me his old Oldsmobile. As usual, I was making money. I had my own paper route, mowed all the neighborhood lawns and worked during the summers for the local ice cream and restaurant shop. I was always working, and I was saving money for college.

My sister Sheila was going to college, and my middle sister Alice was in high school with me. She was a junior when I was a sophomore. It was always understood in our family that we would all go to college. My father was not one of those parents who said: "*Not* getting an education was good enough for me…" Instead he recognized the importance of education and said: "I didn't get it, so you're going to get it."

When it came time for me to decide where to attend college, the only question was how we would afford it because he was paying for Sheila at Boston University, and Alice who now was attending the University of Massachusetts. Fortunately, UMass was a state school with a low tuition so we could afford that for Alice and me.

One thing happened, though, that spoiled an otherwise happy time in my life. The valedictorian of my class was a good friend. He wanted to attend MIT, and we would go to lectures there from time to time. Unfortunately, the day after we finished classes, and before we went to graduation, he killed himself. He cranked up the car and asphyxiated himself with the exhaust. I never knew why he committed suicide. There was a side of him that I never saw because he was introverted, although he played music and he played basketball with me in the church league. I guess he suffered from depression. It was one of those traumatic events that happen in your life that you may never understand but makes you grateful to still be healthy and alive.

I decided to study engineering in college. I applied to MIT and was offered a partial scholarship. I also applied to Union College and received a full scholarship. I applied to the University of Massachusetts, too, and finally went there mainly because it was still less expensive than the other two colleges.

When I looked at what UMass offered, I determined that chemical engineering was the hardest course they had. That's why I took it. I figured that if I didn't succeed at that, I had a lot of less difficult majors to fall back on. I started my classes and found that the basic first-year curriculum was not difficult for me.

I confirmed in my sophomore year to continue in chemical engineering, and I was following some amazing students. Jack Welch, who later headed GE, was two years ahead of me in chemical engineering. Dick Mahoney, who was also two years ahead of me, ended up running Monsanto. Joe Flavin, again, two years ahead of me, would run Singer. Jack Smith, who was a classmate of mine, would lead General Motors. It was fascinating to me that every one of them was first generation Irish. Just like me, they were Boston-Irish families who couldn't afford to have their motivated kids go anyplace else but a state school.

College was difficult at times, but I persevered and my world was becoming much larger. I was taking the long view and called on my self-discipline to pull me through. Two of my strands.

———

Chapter 2

A Single Person With An Idea Can Make A Difference

I received a 3.2 GPA in the first semester of my freshman year, and I was pleased with myself. I wasn't even studying and still did well. I went out for the swimming team and also played tennis. I wanted to join a fraternity, but I wasn't allowed to do so until second semester, so instead I hung out with a lot of engineering students. They became my close friends.

I also continued to make money as I always had. I even took in laundry. Now that I was a second semester freshman, I joined the Sigma Phi Epsilon fraternity, which, coincidentally, was the fraternity of my sister Alice's boyfriend.

In my sophomore year, I ended up with a 2.4 in the first semester and even failed a course. I believe I had a good reason for that failure. I was out for three weeks with the flu along with most everyone else. The flu had decimated the school. The college put beds in the student union to keep everyone together and away from those who had not yet contracted the disease.

Instead of being a terrible situation, we turned it into a fun time. I became the 'president' of *Flu U* and I organized everyone into collecting their codeine terpin hydrate. Instead of taking it as the doctor ordered, we would pool it and enjoy a big codeine party at night.

Despite this setback, I was able to slog my way back. I didn't make the dean's list, which was disappointing, but I garnered a 2.9 GPA. I didn't bask in glory, but I did have a great time.

Between my sophomore and junior year, I traveled to Europe with my cousin Colin who had come to live with my family just before my freshman year. Often he would visit me at school, and we became very close, like brothers. He was working for BF Goodrich and had vacation time, so off we went.

The day we landed in Paris was the same day Charles de Gaulle came to power. There was absolute chaos because the Gaullists were fighting the Communists, and mobs filled the streets. Our plane was the last one to land before authorities shut the airport.

On a dreary day in Paris we were sitting in a sidewalk café - I was 19 and my cousin was 20 - and several people our age came in and we struck up a conversation. They turned out to be the Junior Davis Cup team including Butch Buchholtz, Chuck McKinley and Dennis Ralston. They were in Paris to compete in the French/International tennis tournament. We partied with them for several days and were their guests at the Roland Garros matches. We were wondering how they had all the money they seemed to spend so freely. It became clear when we saw them receive envelopes containing 'expense money' from the head of a company sponsor. They were amateurs and not allowed to take money, so some also was funneled through older women who were 'taking care' of them. It was an eye-opener for me about how the world of sports worked and especially so-called amateur tennis.

After staying in Paris for about a week, we traveled to Geneva and Zurich. We went on to Germany then Holland where we ended up in the red light district in Amsterdam and then on to Brussels. We visited the World's Fair, walking across the fairgrounds, and then under a big structure that looked like a gigantic atom (the *Atomiom*) when a girl called my name. I didn't recognize her, but we struck up a conversation and my cousin looked at me, thinking, "How could Brian possibly know somebody in Brussels?" It turned out that she and I had met at a fraternity party at UMass. She was a fair guide who invited us to hang out with her group. They had been working for about six weeks, knew all the ins and outs of the Fair, and we got to go behind the scenes with them. They took us to terrific parties and we got to know a different side of Brussels than most tourists.

From there we visited my cousin's home in Dagenham, England, and stayed with my aunt and uncle. Unfortunately, my cousin had to return to work as he only had three weeks off, but I went on to Scotland by myself. Then I went to Ireland to meet my relatives.

I landed in Dublin and took a train to the center of Lurgan and then a cab to one of my aunt's houses where I was going to stay. The cab driver knew exactly who I was. "Oh, you're Hugh Thompson's son," he said. Word had gotten around that I was visiting. Truth be told, there weren't a lot of people visiting Northern Ireland at the time, so foreigners stood out.

I learned more about my father's life in Ireland, the house he was brought up in, his friends. I got to meet his sisters and brothers and all of my cousins. One thing that stood out was how much he was admired by his family, much more so than I would have expected. Maybe they thought he had become a rich American.

My parent's 25th wedding anniversary was coming up on July 15, and I wanted to be with them, so I flew home four or five days earlier than I had planned. I took the subway from Logan Airport to Ashmont Station and then took a cab. I didn't want them to see me, so I asked the driver to let me off on the bottom of the hill. Our house was on the top. I had bought them gifts in Shannon before I left Ireland and carried them up the hill and entered the house on the day of their anniversary. They were surprised and overjoyed to see me. I had closed a loop that began in 1938 during their trip to Ireland when I was thought of and my name chosen but not yet conceived.

One of my most important non-academic activities in college was skiing, which I began in my senior year. I joined a group of guys in New Hampshire who were absolute fanatics. That was 1960. The following year, ten of us got a house in Bartlett, New Hampshire, which we used as a base for skiing. Because of our extreme skiing, a mystique grew up around our group and the other skiers called us *The Mountain Men*. I'm not sure how that particular name took hold, but it became a badge of honor, and we were well known in the area.

All throughout New England at the time, there were a lot of ski clubs. Instead of staying in hotels, these clubs took over houses, as we did, which became like combined fraternity/sorority houses. We lived there while skiing, held parties and had a raucous time.

We raced all over New England and won dozens of trophies. In the spring, as the snow receded, we skied on Mt. Washington's Tuckerman Ravine which was known as the Mecca for extreme skiing in the East.

I stayed with this group for about two years until I entered the Navy. My going-away party - at least what I remember of it - included an anchor chained to my leg.

Looking back at that experience, I realize that skiing taught me some lessons that I used later in my business life. For example, in order to be a successful skier you sometimes have to do exactly the opposite of what your body tells you to do – go against your natural instinct.

Let's say you're leaning out over a steep slope, almost a full-fledged cliff. Your body is telling you that you're losing your balance and need to fall back into the mountain. But, the more you stay out over your skis, the better your control. You have to understand and appreciate that you shouldn't always follow your instincts, but think instead about what's really happening. It's about venturing outside of your comfort zone. You're experiencing something that's intellectually correct but physically uncomfortable.

When I graduated in 1960, there weren't a lot of jobs available. I interviewed at many places - Monsanto, DuPont, Allied - and now that I was leaving college, my draft status became 1-A and the military had me in its sights. The Berlin crisis was heating up, men were being drafted, but there were exemptions for some jobs. Companies would tell me: "If you come to our laboratories and do research, we can get you an exemption." I resisted that because

I had been doing lab work for the past three years, and I didn't want to do it anymore. I wanted to get involved in the application of technology.

I really wasn't sure what to do next.

I got an interview with Kendall, which had brands with which I was familiar: Curity diapers, Curad bandages. An old Boston family owned the company, and its textile mills were in the process of shifting to non-woven textiles. That seemed interesting to me, and I interviewed with Ross Whitman who was the head of sales & marketing *and* research in their main location in Walpole, Massachusetts.

He had discovered a process in which he added caustic soda to cotton and created an interlocked web of fibers that could be turned into felt without having to do any weaving or mechanical processing. The material, called *Webril*, exhibited a unique surface that could carry many different kind of liquids. It was used later by the Polaroid camera company as a wet holder for photograph fixer, the little lipstick-like tube that you spread on instant photos to keep them from fading. *Webril* was also used in offset printing to hold ink before transference to paper.

One day, Ross went to the head of Kendall and said, "I've got this spectacular idea. We could develop a home hair permanent kit that carried all the chemicals in these Webril webs. All a woman has to do is remove it from the bag, put the webs in her hair and not have to bother with applying messy liquid chemicals anymore."

Ross met with resistance but was so sure of himself that he said: "Look, if you don't mind, I would like to take a leave of absence and see if there's a market for this product." Bill Forsell, the company president, told him that he could leave along with his patent. Ross did and produced the *Toni* brand home permanent kit, the first of its kind. He eventually sold the company and made a considerable fortune.

But then he did something odd. Ross told the folks at Kendall, "I really love this place and I'd like to come back," so they cut a deal in which he became the head of sales & marketing and research. I thought this was a reasonable combination of roles but have never seen it since then.

Preston Marshall and Art Olsen, who were vice president and director of research, were sitting with me when I told them that I didn't want to do research anymore, but they offered me a job doing research anyway and I took it despite my reservations. It was the first solid job offer I had received since college, and it was $500 a month. That was big money for me, and I couldn't turn it down.

What happened next took me aback. Olsen set up a desk for me in the middle of the lab and gave me a giant book to read about Kendall's policies and procedures. After I finished the book I said: 'What do I do now?'

"What is it that you'd like to do?" he said.

'I've been in college for four years and everybody told me what I had to do every hour, every minute. I'm not used to doing anything on my own,' I said.

"This is research. Go back to your desk. Talk to other people. Find out what's going on here and then come back to us with a plan," he said.

I thought to myself: 'This is crazy.'

After a while, I responded: 'If I'm going to work with textiles, I have to find out what makes them all work and how they interface and how they interlock and their chemical makeups. I'm going to better understand how you produce your products.' So I did just that. I talked to people and returned with a plan. I got samples of every fiber to learn about them. It was pure research.

I became interested in *alginate fiber,* a water soluble fiber made from algae. If you take algae, mix it with a phosphate and spin it, it becomes a fiber. A strong fiber that can be dyed, but the downside is that it becomes a gelatinous mess if water hits it. There was a story going around the office told by the person who produced the alginate. He said that the actor Errol Flynn had bathing suits made out of the material and gave them to women who came to his house for pool parties. I didn't know if the story was true or not but it was amusing. Clearly, there was nothing we could do with alginate fiber, so I got samples of other fibers and subjected them to various processes to see how they reacted.

I had over 70 different fibers, and I did needle punching, in which big punches came down to interlock the fibers. I put fibers through chemical treatments, additive treatments, salt water treatments, whatever I could think of. After all, I saw how Ross had added caustic soda to cotton fibers and came up with the first home permanent kit. Maybe I could come up with something equally valuable.

I was testing Dacron, trying to learn more about the fiber's structure. Dacron is a polyester fiber formed by spinning a liquid at high speeds. It comes out as an interlocked chemical structure but also in that structure are some areas that have not been bound up. It has pieces going every which-way. Dacron fibers have little amorphous sections in them, and what I found was that when they were heated that amorphous part came to the surface and crystallized. It was like the salt on the surface of a pretzel. When you pulled all these fibers together and heated them, the fiber itself shrinks a bit and changes its characteristics. More importantly, the fiber web that I had produced became 20 to 50 times stronger. You could not pull it apart.

At our annual meeting, the board of directors visited the lab so researchers could show what they were doing, and I took them through my findings. I had all of the fibers sitting on little hangers. They were treated in different ways and I had weights on them. I hung a weight on one and it would fall, *boom*. I hung a weight on another and *thunk*. The next one went *bloop*. Then, I showed the Dacron fibers that I treated and they just sat there with a weight five times the others. It didn't tear it. Great showmanship on my part, and everybody was looking at me, saying, "Wow. Isn't that something."

After the meeting I said, 'Ross, what do I do now?'

He said, "What do you mean what do you do? You tell me what you should do."

I said, 'Well, I think it's got great characteristics.'

"Well, what the hell do you think it's going to be good for? Why don't you visit with our sales office, take samples with you and talk to the salesmen and see what they think." So I talked to the salesmen and they came up with a lot of different ideas. The next step was to go to New York with samples and meet with customers who had these characteristics in mind. One customer was an industrial diaphragm manufacturer, and another was a molded brassiere maker.

I returned to the office from the lab to get some more samples, not realizing until I returned that I would have to draw up specifications to produce the fibers and then convince the plant managers to make it. I needed fabric so I could cut pieces of it to send it to the guy who was making brassieres and the other guy for diaphragms. I was only 22 and had no power over the production people to do anything for me. I had to sweet talk them into fitting it into their production schedule. Not only that, but I had to come up with costs and time calculations for how long it would take to produce my samples.

At the same time, I was working with attorneys and Kendall's basic research organization at MIT to file for patents for the processes. It was a lot for a kid my age to handle.

I got the plant to try a production run for the brassieres fabric. Later, they produced diaphragm materials for motor controls using the fibers. The company was getting some value out of my work, but it wasn't until much later that I realized that this was a unique experience. I was there for eighteen months and I had learned everything from the research bench to product development to the sales offices to production, quality control and shipping. Although it didn't happen until after I had left Kendall, I ended up with a dozen patents for useful and valuable permutations of Dacron that DuPont had never considered.

I learned how organizations operated, how they got things done and how the informal structure in companies could make things happen. I saw how people interacted with one another, and how moving from technology to a product takes place in a real company instead of some theory. I learned how you worked with people at each step along the way so that you gained enough credibility that they would help you.

It taught me about the interface between the research and other departments. I learned how you completed actual research, not just talked about it, and how you produced items of value. I learned about costs, budgets and how a product turns profitable.

Perhaps the most important thing I took away from this experience was how successful an organization could be when it respected the ability of an individual to pursue an idea. I'm sure it was because of Ross's influence and how he challenged people to think for themselves and figure out what they should do. He allowed people to take new paths, even make mistakes along the way. It was okay to try and fail. It's a lesson that I've never forgotten.

I had allowed people to help me, an important strand in my red thread. Meanwhile, the draft board was becoming more interested in me and my 1-A status. It was time for me to make a decision about the military and for me to try to control my future instead of having decisions made for me.

———

Chapter 3

An Icelandic Epic

As soon as I learned that I was coming up for the draft, I signed on for Navy flight school as a way of preempting the army from conscripting me. The Navy seemed safer, and after subjecting me to physicals during a six month process, they accepted my application in December 1961. I was to start flight school training in April 1962.

But before I accepted the commitment, I reconsidered my decision and called the recruiter.

'I'm not going to fly,' I told him. He couldn't believe it. Nobody had ever turned down flight school. People would kill to fly Navy, he said. He told me about how much money and time they had spent on me, but my mind was made up, and I had good reasons. Two of my good friends had died flying for the Navy during the six month processing period. One of them missed landing on a carrier and the other was flying a routine patrol when he lost control of his plane. If this happens in peacetime, imagine what could happen if there was a war?

I knew I was committed to being in the Navy so I told the recruiter to find me something else, and he did.

About five days after I would have begun flight school in Pensacola, I began training at OCS, the Officer Candidate School, in Newport, Rhode Island, where they dehumanize you for about three months as they turn you into a fighting machine. I was tested right out of the gate, both physically and psychologically, when we began marching. It should have been a simple exercise, but after three days I got out of bed and fell flat on my face.

The problem stemmed from a ski race at Wildcat Mountain in New Hampshire several months earlier. It was an extremely cold and windy day, and I was traveling very fast into a high speed turn when I lost control. I ended up in the woods, everything was going by at lightning speed as I flipped over and I drove my hip into a rock. The pain was so intense that I passed out. I learned much later that I destroyed the bursa sac in my left hip. Even so, I finished out the skiing season despite the pain.

The Navy trainers were continually accusing me of shirking my duties, deliberately trying to muster out for medical reasons because they couldn't find any reason for my pain.

Fortunately, I caught a break. During the time that I was skiing, I was dating a girl named Kim from Maine. Her former boyfriend (who still thought she was his girlfriend) was the head of the regimental color guard in the class ahead of mine. I knew him from skiing as well. He came to visit me in the barracks, and I told him about not being able to march because I had reinjured my hip and that my superiors didn't believe my story. He suggested that I join the color guard so I didn't have to march to class every day. On the other hand, I would become part of the regimental color guard where I would still march but, overall, it would be less rigorous.

This ploy didn't make a lot of sense to the doctors who were still confused about my complaints about pain. But to me it seemed easier and less stressful than doing the normal everyday drills and exercises you had to endure if you were not in the color guard.

I also swam - I was a collegiate swimmer - which was a low impact exercise for my hip. I was a distance swimmer; I was okay, but I wasn't great. It turned out that our company had two swimmers who had competed in the 1960 Olympics, so we beat all the other companies.

Once you completed eight weeks of grueling training, you were allowed to go off base and wear a set of officer-type uniforms. This was great because the uniforms would help us meet girls in the bars, including some we termed 'debutantes' from Fall River.

Because of the swim team, I was hanging out with a group of men who were interested in diving jobs and they were trying to convince me to look into the three diving programs that the Navy offered.

The first was salvage diving. These divers donned hard hats and salvaged sunken ships and their contents. It was interesting enough but not too exciting. The second was the Underwater Demolition Team or UDT who were charged with attacking the shore and setting mines in enemy waters. Their purview at that time could carry them from three miles to five miles inland, and then the landing parties would come in to continue the job. Essentially, they were the first lead of attack in the area and made it safe for the Marines to land. The third choice was EOD or Explosive Ordnance Disposal, divers who disarmed torpedoes and removed enemy mines as part of the UDT to secure safe entry for other forces. A few years later, these responsibilities were coupled with additional roles and capabilities to form the Navy SEAL teams.

While I was considering these options, the base captain and the head of our company called me in because of my chemical engineering background. They wanted me to become a chemistry professor at the Naval Academy. This seemed mundane to me, and I turned down their offer. I said: 'I'm going to do chemical engineering for the rest of my life. Why would I want to be a professor at the Naval Academy? I joined the Navy to see other parts of the world and do new things...' and while I was talking I realized that I was saying the wrong thing, offending these officers and courting trouble by turning down their offer. Still, I wanted to do something interesting and challenging, so I signed up for EOD. When I told my mother what I was planning to do she said: "Brian, you didn't want to fly because it was too dangerous and now you're disposing of bombs?" She had a point.

The training that followed made my previous training seem easy. We trained in many different places including almost a full year at Key West Naval Base and the Naval Surface Warfare Center in Indian Head, Maryland. In Key West we had six weeks of scuba training along with grueling, physical training. They also gave us academic classes to learn about the effects of diving on the human body.

We had another four weeks of scuba-type diving, but with mixed gas. This equipment allowed you to dive deeper without sound or magnetic signatures. This was followed by six weeks of hard-hat diving. When we finished training we were all fully qualified in every type of diving apparatus that the Navy employed, some of which we were not permitted to discuss publicly.

During my stay in Key West, the closest military base to Cuba, President Kennedy announced that the Navy was placing a blockade around the Soviet ally. The blockade would stay in place until Fidel Castro removed Soviet missiles from the island. During this period of high tension we were training and supporting the Navy patrols. Like everyone else in the country, we didn't know if the Cuban Missile Crisis would lead to war between the United States and the Soviet Union. Fortunately, Castro and Soviet leader Nikita Khrushchev backed down.

The next phase was weapon's training and that lasted about eight months. We were checked out on every weapon that was made from the Civil War, including those employing cannonballs, through those deployed to that time, June 1963. We were even trained on the *Davy Crockett*, a personally-delivered tactical nuclear weapon, as well as Titan II Multiple Reentry Vehicles, an extremely complex nuclear device.

By the time I was done with all of my training there were only six of us left from the 85 that started. Some guys rolled back and others went elsewhere, and we had two others who joined us from a previous class. The high dropout rate reminded me of my chemical engineering class. Of 65 students, only eight of us graduated from that course of study.

Our graduating class was then deployed all over the world, and the top of the class had their choice. Even though I had first choice, I surprised my colleagues when I chose to go somewhere for which very few opted: Iceland. There was a U.S. Naval Station in Keflavik (now a NATO base) and clearly it was the most remote and least desired among my class, especially to those who were married. To me, though, it was different and exciting.

It was just the kind of place that I wanted.

About 260,000 people inhabited the volcanic island. I was on the island just three days - I had not even begun my job - when I got a preview of how crazy my stay in Iceland would become. Because most of the officers' lives revolved around the O Club, my BOQ neighbors introduced me to the weekend routine there. When I walked into the club I saw a guy who was really drunk, playing slot machines. I looked over and saw that he was a lieutenant commander with a cross on his uniform - a chaplain. He was almost incoherent and yet was playing the slot machine. As I watched this show, I said to myself, 'This is going to be a wild tour.' Later that evening, I heard a *thunk* in the room above mine in the BOQ. The chaplain had fallen out of bed.

We did a great deal of diving around the island which didn't offer very deep waters. One of our jobs was to disarm mines left over from the German mining of the North Atlantic. These mines would come up in fishing nets, but very often when the local fishermen were having a slow day, they would fish in the restricted waters and intentionally bring up test dummy bombs and other leftover materiel so they could receive compensation from the government for a loss of one day's fishing. They would get paid for the time they waited for us to respond to their location. After a few episodes, I put an end to this practice by not responding to anything but legitimate mines that were caught in nets. Eventually, the fishermen learned not to call us unless they had a genuine mine or some other dangerous device.

I also had the opportunity to actually seek out and destroy old British mines left after World War II. The Codfish Wars between the British and Icelanders, both claiming fishing rights to the same piece of ocean, gave us an opening for removing those mines.

The Brits pushed their case by fishing within ten miles of the Icelandic coast. The Icelanders had one Coast Guard boat with a 40 millimeter cannon, and they would fire at the British vessels. Trying to come to an armistice, the British, as a goodwill gesture, offered to clear all of the mines that they had left in the fjords after

World War II when the two nations began their disagreements. Fishing rights aside, the British were still unhappy with the Icelanders because they allowed German submarines into the eastern part of the island during World War II at the same time that the British operated a patrol plane base on the southwestern part of the island.

I went minesweeping for two weeks with the British, and it was a great adventure. We swept fjords in the north and east and sixteen mines came up. These were 500-pound moored mines. Really powerful. We decided as a practical matter that the best thing to do with some of these mines was to pack them with C4 explosives and blow them up. We told the Icelanders that it was our way of disposal, but it really was our way to make a dramatic point so they could see that we were doing our job.

We didn't explode all of the mines, though. Some we just sank in very deep water, but the true entertainment came because the shape of the fjords amplified the explosive sounds and carried it for long distances. It was extremely loud and made a strong impression on the Icelandic citizens and their sheep.

I had a great experience sailing with the Brits. I got along with them because anytime on a mine sweeper when two officers got together they unofficially could open a bar. It was a tradition. Also, they never wore uniforms, just sweaters, which to me was very cool. It was a different way of operating from ours, and we had a lot of laughs. Being an EOD diver often on board their mother ship, *The Reclaim*, that held the deep diving record of 462 feet, was a rush.

Off-duty life was special as well. Besides the work and nightlife, I enjoyed the unique outdoor recreation that Iceland offered. I climbed Mount Hekla, and I skied on the glaciers. I flew sail planes and set foot on a new island that was created offshore by an active volcano.

The most important event that happened during my tour didn't happen on the island but when I returned to the States after six months so I could requalify for my deep-diving certification.

For safety reasons, we were only allowed to requalify where the Navy had a decompression chamber and the nearest one for me was at Indian Head, Maryland.

Once I got to the States, I needed a way to get from Washington, DC to Indian Head, so I called one of my friends whose wife was working in Washington. She belonged to a carpool that went between Indian Head and the capital. In the car was a beautiful woman named Mary Ann Selby. I was taken by how pretty, demure and fascinating she was, but nothing went further until I was back in Indian Head about two weeks later, and I got an invitation to a friend's 'wetting down' party there. By then, I was a lieutenant junior grade. I needed a date for the party and asked my friend's wife to call the girl from the carpool and see if she would accompany me. Mary Ann said that she would go as my date.

About two weeks after we met, after three dates, we attended an out-of-town wedding together, and Mary Ann's father and mother picked us up at the airport upon our return. Her mother was sitting in front and we were in the backseat. I asked her father for his daughter's hand in marriage just as we entered their driveway. He just sat there and didn't utter a word. I was worried that he was holding back his reply because he disapproved. Her mother said: "Bern! Didn't you hear what Brian said?" It turned out that he wasn't being dismissive, he just hadn't heard a word I said.

Mary Ann said 'yes,' and I gave her a ring that I had bought at a jeweler next to my dad's office in Boston. We were engaged. Three days later, President Kennedy was shot, which was very sad for us not just because he was the president but because my dad and the Kennedy family were close after he had helped Jack Kennedy's career by taking on the St. Lawrence Seaway debate.

I had become friendly with the family earlier that year as well. On one occasion, my dad was meeting with Ted Kennedy and he invited me to join the family at Stowe, Vermont for a skiing weekend. It was a special experience for a lieutenant JG at Indian Head, rolling into Butler Aviation at National Airport and getting on *The Caroline*, their family aircraft.

As we taxied out, the pilot abruptly stopped the plane and announced that the president's press conference had begun. We pulled off the taxiway, and the crew brought out a television from one of the plane's cabinets. In those days having a television in your plane was rare and we watched the president conduct his press conference. It was Thursday, and this was a normal weekly event for this family. For me, it was a once-in-a-lifetime experience.

Ted wasn't with us on the plane, but on board was his wife Joan, Bobby and Ethel, Secretary of Defense Bob McNamara and his wife and their son. Joe Tydings, who was a Maryland senator, his wife, and two friends of Bobby, Dave Hackett and Dean Markham were on board. It was the Washington Birthday weekend. When we got to Stowe, they stayed at The Lodge; I stayed at a nearby private home. Ted showed up later with several of Joan's friends. They were recently married and didn't have any kids. We partied and skied all weekend.

Following the tragic Kennedy funeral week in Washington, I returned to Iceland and told Mary Ann: 'When I finish my tour in May, I'll come back. We'll get married and then we'll go off to another station but I don't know where we'll be going.' I had another year in the Navy, and I was kind of a free spirit. Mary Ann was bright-eyed, living with her family and liked the idea of adventure, so she was game.

The hardest thing for me was to return to Iceland without Mary Ann. Fortunately, when I got there I was able to call her every night through the 'operator friendly' hotline to Andrews Air Force Base in Maryland who then would connect us. Despite our every-night phone conversations, neither of us could remember what the other one looked like. We had photos to remind each other, but that was all.

We had known each other for such a short time, but I was ready to set a wedding date. During the third week of December I called Mary Ann from Iceland and said that I decided to bag my planned trip to the Olympics in Innsbruck. I said: 'I'll be coming back to see you in a couple of months, so let's get married then. If I'm still in Iceland after we're married, you can get a housing allowance back home. That will give us a little more money to start out our life, because you can still live with your parents.' Unbelievably, and on such short notice, she agreed.

On Sunday, February 2, 1964, I arrived in Washington where we got reacquainted amid the excitement, happiness, concern and pride that goes with an impending wedding. Six days later, on February 8th, we were married.

During that week, I was tying up loose ends and had gone to the Navy Bureau of Personnel in D.C. and said: "I'm here because I'm due to get orders in May, and I just wonder where you're thinking of sending me."

The Navy was planning to send me to Indian Head, but I balked. I didn't think it was a good idea for a newly-married couple to live in the wife's hometown. I liked my in-laws, but I thought a young couple should have their own space. EOD was a special designation with 250 slots for 75 officers in the entire Navy. I had some negotiating power, and I was able to wrangle a deployment to the Naval Air Station in Alameda, California. I had to agree to an additional year of service, but I thought it was good deal considering that they could have sent me to Vietnam. I was taking the long view. The hardest part was explaining to Mary Ann's parents why I turned down a posting near their house.

———

Chapter 4

Bomb Disposal Amid The Fireworks

As I was leaving Iceland, we bought a fairly inexpensive car, a Chevy Impala convertible, and were preparing to drive to Alameda for my two-year tour. On the way, we visited my sister and her husband in Gulfport, Mississippi. We stayed at the Montelone Hotel in New Orleans, visited the Grand Canyon and Yosemite Park, and somewhere on that trip my daughter was conceived.

When we arrived in Alameda, they assigned me to live on base and only had available substandard housing with two little bedrooms, a living room and a kitchen. We had no furniture, appliances or anything else. I picked out furnishings that they had available on the base, and it was pretty sad stuff. They delivered a rug and Mary Ann was surprised by its appearance. She said to the delivery person: "That's a mat. Where's the rug?"

We were there only a few weeks - we arrived shortly after Memorial Day, 1964 - when Mary Ann exhibited morning sickness.

Alameda was an active base because of the Vietnam War. Ships that home-ported there included the *Coral Sea*, the *Midway, Ranger* and the *Enterprise*, the world's first nuclear carrier. In fact, the whole San Francisco Bay area was very busy with naval activity. Across the Bay at Hunters Point was a large ship repair facility. Further up the Bay in Concord was a naval magazine which stored and shipped weapons. Vallejo housed a large submarine base.

As an EOD guy, I was part of the weapons department. If there were any problems, any issues involving explosives, I was in charge. Because of my security clearance, I was also available to transport higher level weapons, including nuclear devices.

The author's diving team was composed of Lt. David Kweder (top left), CPO Hartman (middle), Author (top right) and 2nd Class Torpedoman Carrier (bottom left), First Class Ordnanceman Pugh (middle), 1st Class Ordnanceman Hackworth (bottom right).
Author's collection.

On July 4th - I had been there about six weeks - a man called the base because he saw a torpedo floating in his backyard off Bay Farm Island near Oakland Airport. We inquired if he had been drinking, but he insisted that he was sober and the sighting was real. From what we had later determined, it was a torpedo that had been fired during World War II at an enemy submarine seen off-shore. In general, torpedoes that missed their target would float for a while before sinking. This one apparently sank in the mud and came out of the gunk some 20 years later. What amazed us was that it had floated all the way through San Francisco's Golden Gate, through the shipping channels, all the way over to this particular island without anyone spotting it. This 20-foot long torpedo carried about 500 pounds of explosives.

Normally, we would either blow up old explosives in place or gingerly transport them to a designated site on the base and blow them up. Obviously we couldn't blow it up where it was nor could we transport it safely. The torpedo had been made 20 years ago and was too sensitive to move.

We were familiar with this model torpedo because there was a very similar one sitting in the bone yard that we had used to train on during school. It was typical of those carried during the war by United States diesel submarines.

We decided to dismantle it where we found it – in waist high water right next to the caller's backyard. We tethered it, and took turns working on it. We disassembled it and removed the detonator which was the most dangerous component. We then removed the booster. We continued to dismantle the torpedo, deliberately, slowly and by the book.

We finished at 7:00 p.m. and brought in a crane and our truck so we could take it back to the base to blow up the explosives it contained. With the detonator and other devices removed, it now was safe to transport.

The local authorities let a photographer onto the scene and we were on the front page of *The Los Angeles Times* and *The New York Times*. Just as we were lifting the torpedo for transport, fireworks had commenced at Oakland Airport. I found out later that Mary Ann was crazy with worry because we didn't have cell phones in those days and she didn't know where the hell we were or what was going on. All she heard were explosions. She didn't know if it was us or the festivities.

As I did in Iceland, I enjoyed my time in San Francisco and continued to learn how to 'work the system.' As usual, our diving team made deals to expedite our comfort and fun while serving the country. When any of our EOD or UDT diving teams were assigned to ships that put into nearby ports, the last thing any of them wanted to do was stand duty on the vessel. They wanted to come ashore and be a part of our team until they deployed again. We made a deal with anyone who wanted to leave their ship to issue them special orders to join our team when their ship was in port or in one of the repair facilities. It cost them a 20-pound tin of coffee for each man who came over. We would then work out together, run together, and they would dive with our team whenever we could free up time to go diving.

We would travel to Monterrey where I had a deal with the harbormaster to use his picket boat, a 45-foot powerboat that was suited for deep water, so we could perform our requalification diving. Or, we would go to Point Reyes where the Coast Guard would loan us a boat for diving off the Point. While diving, we would bring up abalone and trade them with the fisherman for salmon and crab. On the way back to the base we would stop at Bodega Bay where there was a Japanese group farming blue oysters. We bartered and ate well.

Mary Ann was from a family raised in Solomons Island, Maryland on Chesapeake Bay. She was especially fond of seafood and crabs, and asked me to bring back a few dozen crabs on my next trip. On our next excursion I asked a fisherman for as many crabs as he had, and he said that he had less than a dozen. I traded him some abalone. I figured the small number of crabs wouldn't make much of a meal, but I carried them home anyway sight-unseen in a burlap bag and handed them to Mary Ann with an apology. 'I'm sorry, honey. They only had 11 crabs. That's all I could get.'

"It probably isn't worth heating the water to boil them," she said.

'Well, come on out there and look at them anyway,' I replied.

Her scream filled the neighborhood. She had never seen such large creatures. She thought I was playing a prank on her, but both of us being from the East Coast, we were not familiar with the huge Dungeness crabs which are much, much larger than the Chesapeake Blue crabs we had eaten at home. She cooked the crabs one at a time and picked about 2 -1/2 quarts of meat from them. It was a fine introduction to West Coast seafood.

We had coffee from sailors who wanted to go ashore and had abalone to trade from our dives. What our team didn't have was real money to buy equipment that we needed to do our jobs. We had to scrounge.

On one occasion, we needed to build a high-pressure air compressor system to fill the diving tanks. How did we do it? We took abalone and coffee to the men in the maintenance facility to trade for aviator oxygen bottles that we could convert and add to our issued scuba gear. Then we went over to Oakland to the Naval Supply Center. We would drop in there once every couple of weeks because they had material from all over the Pacific, everything that was no longer being used or that had been incorrectly ordered or whatever. We would rummage through this facility as if it was a junkyard, but it was not a real junkyard because it had a lot of material that we could 'requisition' to build whatever we needed. Eventually, we were able to construct an air compressor system to fill our scuba tanks. I also scavenged parts and put together a washer and dryer for Mary Ann.

All of the police and fire department divers in the San Francisco Bay Area learned very quickly where they could get their tanks filled. We got to know them well, which was good and bad. When they had a problem, like some idiot with a cannonball or somebody with a hand grenade or a doll that they thought contained explosives, we were the guys on call and we had to respond. The worst calls were plane crashes. You didn't know what grisly situation you would encounter.

All in all, though, it was a great tour. We loved being in San Francisco, but I also knew that I had to line up some work once I got out of the Navy.

I had already taken some correspondence courses because I wanted to learn more about business. My interest in business was piqued when I was dating a woman whose father was an engineer like me, but he also had attended business school. When I met him, he had a 28-room house in Philadelphia with butlers, maids, gardeners, cooks and a chauffeur. That got me to thinking that there might be more to engineering than slide rules and calculators.

I signed up at the University of California in Berkeley, which had an extension school in San Francisco, for a course in managerial accounting. I had heard that managerial accounting was the heart of business, but I didn't know much beyond that.

The professor, Clancy Houghton, was a partner in an accounting firm in San Francisco and a graduate of Harvard Business School. A woman in the class owned a flower shop. Another student ran a well-known crab restaurant, Castiglione's, on Fisherman's Wharf. He was taking the course to get a better handle on his restaurant's books.

Prof. Houghton encouraged me to apply to Harvard Business School, so I took a crack at writing the application and thought I had done a decent job of it. At the same time, I called my father: 'I realize that this is an awkward kind of a question, but do you know anybody at Harvard?' My father and mother came to visit and they introduced Mary Ann and me to Joe O'Donnell who was running the labor program at Harvard Business School. He came to my house for dinner. He was most encouraging perhaps because of my labor-oriented family.

Later, Prof. Houghton invited Mary Ann and me to dinner at his house, and I brought my written application to show him. When our wives went off to another room, he proceeded to tear the whole paper apart.

One of the essay questions on the application was: "What are the three things that you think are most important for us to consider?" I had written that I took the hardest course in college, had succeeded with reasonable grades, had a research job at Kendall … and he interrupted me abruptly.

"Wrong, wrong, all wrong! There isn't a person applying to Harvard Business School who didn't finish at the top of his class in whatever the hell he was trying to do, and most of them are engineers. They don't really care that you were the best chemical engineer in your class, and furthermore, a lot of people do a lot of seemingly important things in their first job. It doesn't set you apart. You know what? You're a bomb disposal guy. You lived in Iceland. You have patents. Think about it. You've got people reading application after application and they're all pretty much the same, and then one of them says to the other, "Hey, did you see this guy who was a bomb disposal expert?"

It had never occurred to me, but he was right. My experiences really did set me apart from everyone else who was applying. I made the changes and submitted my application. I had heard that if I didn't receive a written test score above a certain number they wouldn't consider me no matter how different my experience was compared to others. I was worried but took the exam anyway and scored above the cutoff number. About three weeks later, I received my acceptance letter.

It changed my life completely.

My main concern now was money. I was getting out of the Navy in May, had no income, and we had a baby. How could I afford tuition, food and an apartment? The G.I. Bill would give us about $135 a month to help pay for our expenses, but I needed to get a job before school started in the fall.

I was invited to be in the wedding party of Mike Sheridan, an EOD friend who was attending Boston University Law School. His soon-to-be father-in-law, Ray Rich, was chairman of McCall's Corporation, which owned the magazine of the same name. They had other holdings as well. He had done a lot of business in Canada, and he was partners in Canadian Hydrocarbons with a man named David Williams who would later become an important figure in my life.

Mary Ann and I were able to make it back from the West Coast just in time for the wedding, which took place in Nantucket. The bride's father owned homes everywhere, two in Maine, a ranch in Arizona, a house in Philadelphia, a castle in Ireland and two houses on Nantucket. It was a wedding that you might see featured in magazines. They took attendees by boat from Hyannis at 9 a.m., and offered them breakfast and Bloody Mary's during the crossing.

When the attendees arrived in Nantucket, we, the ushers, met them and walked them to the Episcopal church for the marriage ceremony. After the wedding, everyone walked back to the boat where the entire wedding party met them as they walked over the brow and they held the reception on board. Afterwards, some Nantucket residents got off and the rest of us were taken back to Hyannis. We partied all the way across with bands playing on both decks. The newly-married couple changed out of their formal clothes into Levi cutoffs and ran down the pier and onto his 52-foot Pacemaker. They climbed up to the flying bridge and sailed away as everyone watched and listened to the band play *Red Sails in the Sunset*.

While the wedding and party were dazzling to us, the real world beckoned and I still needed a job before I began school in the fall. I had applied to many different companies and was offered a position at Monsanto Research Labs in Cambridge. They knew that I was slated to attend Harvard Business School, but they wanted to hire me anyway, for which I was grateful.

Monsanto had two contracts: one of which was an electro-chemical contract from the National Institutes of Health and the other from the Defense Department. I was just what they were looking for because I had the EOD experience and a COSMIC TOP SECRET (which was a NATO security clearance level) for the DoD job, the goal of which was to find a means of destroying nerve gas by using a chemical reaction.

For the NIH job, I was assigned to a project seeking an electro-chemical couple that would use human blood to power a fuel cell, which then could be implanted in the chest cavity to power an artificial heart. This was around the time that heart surgeon Dr. Michael DeBakey was working on his human heart transplantation and artificial heart. I prepared research reports on both projects.

When I began HBS that fall, I realized that the case study method was the perfect way for me to learn. You didn't need to write a thesis, but instead you engaged in open classroom discussions. It was like being back at my family's dinner table where you had to defend your ideas. I didn't like to write things down, but I liked to work with people. I enjoyed arguing logically with others in a class and reaching a decision. There were no right or wrong answers most of the time. I also liked that in the case studies they inserted lots of information and you had to figure out what was important and what was irrelevant. You learned how to prioritize. Case studies were also compelling lessons in leadership because corporate power was something you saw exuding from different parts of these cases. You saw how power could be used or misused.

One of the great professors, somebody that everybody wanted to have, was Roland Christensen. He was an absolute master of the case method. He could get you engaged, and then he'd say, "But is it justified for a drug company to make such large profit margins? Do you think it's right for a chief executive to be getting a huge salary if *this* is all he's doing," or, "Do you think it's right that these healthcare organizations…" and he would go on challenging us about the ethics of business. It was fabulous and so relevant to business on all levels.

What was really striking, although we didn't realize it at the time, was that Christensen was far ahead of his time. The case study system of teaching most often stressed success measured by profit and loss. If you made the right decision, you likely made money. The wrong decision, and you likely lost money. Christensen underscored again and again that there was more to running a successful business than just profit and loss. Now in business schools they're bringing balance to teaching business ethics along with financial success factors. Strong ethics have always been a part of my business decisions, and it was partly shaped by my time at HBS.

In this type of pull-push, case study environment, I flourished. I was in the top ten to 15 percent, although I never saw myself as an academic.

There were other professors who made an impression on me. One was General George Doriot. He taught a course called *Production*, but it wasn't about production at all. He'd start out by showing you how to read a newspaper to get the most out of the stories. Unfortunately, he stopped teaching just before I got there, but his reputation and imprint on the other parts of the HBS curriculum spurred me to look at the psychological side of business. What about the human side of production? Why do you produce a particular product? Doriot was always asking fundamental questions. Spectacular. People loved to come to class because he was commanding yet passionate and engaging.

During the first year, you were up to your tush in alligators because you were convinced that you were going to washout in the first two weeks. And everybody else was convinced that they were going to washout, too; it was a very intense environment. Once you got through the first year, though, the next big decision was what to do for the summer. The students who were single could go to Europe or whatever else they wanted to do. I wasn't going to go waltzing off to California or anywhere else because I had a wife and child.

I looked around for jobs in the New York and Boston area. I knew that I would have to make a decision by March or April. Because of the work I had done with Kendall, and my chemical engineering background, the best offer that I received was from Celanese. It was a well-respected, large fiber company, as well as a chemical company. Their headquarters were at 522 Fifth Avenue in New York City, which turned out to be prophetic because I later worked in that same building three different times for three different companies.

It was also the place where I learned a life-changing lesson about dysfunctional leadership.

———

Chapter 5

Can You Encourage Entrepreneurship In A Large Corporation?

In the summer of 1967, I packed up Mary Ann and our daughter Christi and headed for New York City. Mary Ann was in the throes of losing a pregnancy, so between that and moving it was a very unsettled time for us.

We didn't have an apartment lined up, but I was looking. We stayed at a friend's apartment on 70th Street on the East Side. I also had a Pan Am pilot friend who lived in Flushing, Queens, and we stayed at his place while he was out of town for several weeks.

Finally, we found a rental in Darien, Connecticut. For most of the summer we lived there, and I commuted to New York City. I thought that was a good idea, because it gave me the opportunity to find out if I liked to commute by train.

Celanese was headed up by a strong-willed, German-American chemist named Harold Blancke. He was the company chairman and CEO and convinced that their future - because they were making synthetic fibers - was in obtaining reliable feedstocks for the fibers. He was playing golf one day and met the owner of Pontiac Refinery in Arkansas. Without consulting anyone, Harold decided to buy the refinery. He did so without conducting any meaningful due diligence. If he had, he would have realized that every scrap of their product was already pre-contracted for 15 years. All the material that we needed - cyclic oligomers - was already promised to others.

He thought of himself as a competent 'deal guy' and proven CEO, so he continued making acquisitions even though they weren't fully thought out. Another of his deals concerned a new, state-of-the-art pulp mill up in Prince Rupert, British Columbia. He bought the mill so his company would have access to what he believed was the cellulose to produce viscose fibers. It was a sound idea on paper, because we needed cellulose for the North Carolina facility, but transportation costs from Prince Rupert were astronomically high and diminished the benefits of owning the mill. He sunk about $90 million into the acquisition.

He had made these purchases before I arrived and one of the projects given to me immediately upon my arrival was to be part of a team tasked to justify the Pontiac Refinery and Prince Rupert acquisitions. Our success would mean that the boss would not be embarrassed by the fact that these were terrible acquisitions.

That was one of my early introductions to the folly of corporate politics. Unfortunately, such behavior was not unusual considering that diversification was in vogue at this time. The business intelligentsia held that a competent manager could manage *any* type of business - and the more the merrier. Certainly, this wasn't always the case.

No one ever came out and said to us, "we need you to make the boss look good," but we all figured out that was what they wanted from our team. They couched it by saying: "We're looking to try to improve the economics." Clearly, the president had committed some big errors, he wouldn't admit it, and no one would tell him that he was wrong. There was a pattern here of failed deals, but nobody would confront the perpetrator.

Even more egregious, perhaps, was when the chairman bought a Convair aircraft so he could commute to North Carolina and New York City from his home in Florida. One of our projects was to show how this purchase made economic sense for the company by filling the plane Monday morning and Friday night with other employees who needed to travel between New York City and North Carolina. Presumably, this would save airfare. The plane had 21 seats, but my analysis showed that breakeven would require 72 seats. No one ever responded to my findings.

The experience left an impression on me about my coming life in business. I couldn't fathom how a company could continue to have a management that did these kinds of dumb and sometimes dishonest actions. How did the guy with the biggest ego end up running the place and then try to make it his little playpen irrespective of the business logic of what he was doing? I'm sure he got there because he was able to convince the board of his competency, a tactic sometimes called 'managing upward.' Sometimes, the guy with the biggest voice or the loudest attitude moves to the top. I understood how that could happen in politics, but it shouldn't happen in business. It isn't fair to the investors or employees.

I saw many division heads who were really smart and could run the company better, but they hadn't been at the right place at the right time to get the top job.

Commuting from Darien to New York City convinced me of a couple of things. It was reasonable to ride the train in the morning, because you could read three newspapers, do your paperwork, prepare for the day, and, when you arrived, you could hit the ground running. The downside was when you had to leave a meeting early because you had to catch the 6:17 or the 5:47 p.m. train. Hoards of people were running for the train with you. Many of them would be so stressed and wiped out from their jobs - and the long train commute - that they would sit stoically in coach cars not wanting to communicate with anyone around them. Others immediately headed for the bar car where they drank and played cards. Sometimes they would drink so heavily that they missed their stops. I have nothing against drinking, but some folks would perform this drinking ritual every day and after a while I didn't want to be around them. It wasn't the kind of life that I wanted.

All in all, though, it was a pleasant summer. Darien was a good environment for our daughter who was almost three years old. Mary Ann had had her first taste of living in New York City and she liked it. We both enjoyed being there, even though we had gone through the tragedy of losing a pregnancy.

When summer ended, I was back at Harvard Business School. The second year was very different from the first. I was not panicked about whether I was going to make it or not. I had become more confident in my ability to participate successfully in the course work. I took investment banking and lending and two doctoral seminars as well, which was pretty unusual for most students. One course was called *Change; Its Social, Psychological and Management Implication.* It was a unique course taught by an industrial psychologist, Renato Tagiuri, who was on the human behavior faculty at the school. His course was about the management of change, which was something that I wanted to better understand. I saw it as vital to many aspects of business. The other session was called *Management of Highly Diversified Companies,* and was especially meaningful after my summer experience. It was taught by Norm Berg.

During my second year, we also had to produce a research paper and I chose to do one about Monsanto. Along with a friend, we found a Monsanto division - the New Enterprise Division - and the question we posed was: "Can you encourage entrepreneurship in a large corporation?"

From my job at Monsanto in 1966, I knew of the establishment of a New Enterprise Division headed by a unique scientist named Dick Gordon. He had received doctorate degrees from both Harvard and MIT in the same year. He was a backfield coach under head football coach Herman Hickman at Yale, and a concert violinist. He had previously headed up Monsanto's basic research labs, where he produced *Astroturf.* He also had a hand in developing *Vitasoy,* a drink that was created for people in developing countries who had no other source of protein.

As a result of his efforts, Dr. Gordon was rewarded by being given his own division designed to highlight the company's ability to bring entirely new products to market which were unrelated to Monsanto's main divisional businesses.

I arranged to meet with Dr. Gordon to tell him about our research project and to ask if we could focus our paper on his division. He had a huge house in the Westmoreland District of St. Louis. When I entered his home, he was sitting in the corner of his living room with his speakers blasting Bartok. He was poised at a TV tray, writing an application to involve Monsanto in the Model Cities Program in Baltimore, St. Louis and Minneapolis. He was a true renaissance man. He also appreciated our idea and gave us the go-ahead. The paper covered many issues, including equity ownership and compensation. Our research took three months to complete, and its conclusion was that there was no way to reward entrepreneurs in large, diversified companies. For this reason, it was difficult if not impossible to accommodate entrepreneurs in such business structures.

Although the paper afforded me a diversion, it was time again to tackle the nagging question: What should I do after school? This time it wouldn't just be a summer-type job because I would graduate and be ready for a permanent position. A lot of companies were at HBS trying to hire graduates because of the school's cachet. I was feeling pretty positive about my graduation rank, the top 15 percent of the class. The top 10 percent were the Baker Scholars. I was proud of my accomplishment considering my lack-luster performance as an undergraduate.

I was fortunate to receive a job offer from McKinsey & Company. It was a consultancy that everyone wanted to join because of their reputation and prestige. It helped that the firm was always interested in HBS graduates. Our class was about 700 people, and McKinsey that year took 14 from our group. At the time, McKinsey had about 400 professional staff and their predominant education backgrounds were MBAs from Harvard Business School. It wasn't any surprise that they took 14 of us; the only surprise was that they were interested in me.

I wanted to work for McKinsey, but didn't want to be in the New York office. I knew that was their headquarters, and the flywheel of the firm, but I wanted them to consider me for the Washington office because of the importance of government to companies. I knew Washington reasonably well, and I knew the Capitol Hill folks and others. To me, there was a gap between how corporations felt about government and how government people felt about corporations. This gap led to misunderstandings which led to problems for corporations. The government affected everything companies did, but many corporate leaders didn't fully appreciate it.

I felt passionate about getting into the public sector side of McKinsey as an attempt to bridge that gap. This idea seems better understood in current day commerce, but at that time even forward-thinking companies like McKinsey did not fully accept the powerful impact that government had on business.

Even so, McKinsey had a fairly robust office in Washington because they were working with the Defense Department on planning and budgeting. They were working with the Department of Housing and Urban Development, Labor Department, Transportation Department and the Post Office on projects, trying to implement more business concepts into their management and decision making.

I began the first of three intensive interviewing cycles. My first cycle took place at Harvard. The recruiters were HR people, and they talked about McKinsey to our group. They had so many Harvard Business School graduates that one of the key directors of the firm, Ron Daniel, had become head of a team that was watching over that year's recruitment activity. They hosted a dinner at the Harvard Club with breakout sessions where I had more interviews. They invited wives so that everyone could meet them.

The next cycle, a continuation of the culling process, took place on campus again, and it ended with a 'yes' or 'no' decision by both sides. My final interview was with a newly-minted director named Lou Gerstner who later became president of American Express, Chairman and CEO of Reynolds and finally CEO of IBM. I made the cut, and they sent me to the Washington office to meet the people there because they would make the final decision about hiring me.

Just before that, however, the firm had me meet with an industrial psychologist which I found to be a fascinating exercise. Its purpose was to obtain a third-party opinion about my suitability to work, let alone succeed, in the consultancy's highly competitive, ego-drenched environment that was McKinsey & Company.

The psychologist practiced in Philadelphia, so I flew from Harvard and spent the day with him. It was a long and tedious interview process with many questions and even some Rorschach tests. He asked me questions like: "Would you rather make sausages, eat sausages or sell sausages?" Despite these seemingly frivolous questions, his probing was designed to penetrate my psyche. At the end of the day, I found it to be an epiphanic experience, linking together and bringing forth for the first time facets of my personality that I thought were disparate. It presented me with a fresh perspective on how and why I acted certain ways and thought the way I did.

At the end of the grueling experience, he said, "I'll tell you what I've found, because this is what I'm going to tell McKinsey, but I will tell you now. First, clearly, you're a fit." He added, "There's no question in my mind about that. You're intense, but you're buttoned up. You're smart. You have enough stability in your personal life to be able to put up with the McKinsey climate."

He continued: "As you went through your life, whether it was the athletics that you got involved in, becoming a Navy EOD Diver or that you chose to be a chemical engineer, you kept returning to the importance of controlling where you were going. You wanted to make sure that if you didn't succeed in what you were trying to do, you had a fallback position so you could dictate where you were going next."

He was on target, and one of the first to identify part of my Red Thread.

I had joked that even when I was engaged in bomb disposal I was pretty much in control. I told him that when you were in bomb disposal and worked in teams, you had to depend upon each other so you had to trust each other. I said, 'Think about this...You're in a hardhat, you're doing a deep-sea dive, your chief petty officer is in control of the compressor that's on the deck and an enlisted guy is holding your lifeline and air hose. If you're an abrasive jerk junior officer in the Navy, it was easier for any of them to do you in than it was for the Army lieutenant who gets shot in the back. All they'd have to do is stop the air compressor or bring you up too quickly and you were done for. Not only did you want to have control, but you had better be damn good in relating to the people around you or you're not going to be alive.'

I always believed that you can be dependent on someone but still control that dependence and understand the risks. (Again, two more of my red thread strands.) It wasn't a question of being sensitive to other people's feelings, as much as it was to understand what you were doing. I wasn't the nice guy who brought all the sides together and then tried to get an answer. Sometimes you had to be a tough guy in many ways if you really believed in what you were doing - if you were confident. How could you win the day, convince others that you're doing the right thing, if you were not confident?

The psychologist said that because of my experiences and beliefs he knew that I would perform well in the McKinsey environment. They often had small, two or three-person teams, assigned to a client. You were always exploring ideas with each other, sometimes arguing and disagreeing. If there was mutual respect among team members, even if discussions turned heated, teams could invariably solve the client's problems and gain their commitment to act on the recommendations.

This experience ended up being a beneficial self-examination, but with the assistance of a professional. It helped me to accept the job because the psychologist assured me that I could succeed in McKinsey's environment. It also helped McKinsey give me the green light.

Next, I traveled to meet the Washington office crew. Mary Ann and I were put up in the Watergate Hotel which was high cotton for us. She visited her folks who lived fairly close and I went into the office. I interviewed with the partners, including the managing partner, John Garrity. He struck me as smart and capable. His brother was a judge in Boston, the same Judge W. Arthur Garrity who was involved in the school busing controversies. John and I were sitting in my final interview, looking out his window at 17th and Pennsylvania, when all of a sudden the city started burning. It was 1968 and riots were breaking out following the shooting of Martin Luther King, Jr. on April 4th. Mary Ann was supposed to pick me up, but Washington was in absolute chaos. Finally, she was able to weave her way through the turmoil and we spent the evening together with mixed emotions. On one hand, we were relishing this stellar professional opportunity before me. On the other, it was heartbreaking and sad to watch the city and the nation fumbling with the societal issues of the time.

I got the job and the offer was $16,000 a year. I figured that I could pay back all of my school loans in five years or so. It was my first permanent job, and I would stay at McKinsey for the next nine years.

———

Chapter 6

Client, Firm And Self

Two McKinsey associates were living in Orleans Village, a townhouse development in Alexandria, Virginia, just outside of Washington, DC, where we worked. On their suggestion Mary Ann and I checked it out and found that it would work for us. Having a three-bedroom apartment would be perfect because our daughter Christi would have her own room, and we would have a spare room in case our family wanted to visit. The commute was much easier than going from Darien to New York. There was a bus that dropped me off a couple of blocks from my office.

My first assignment was being part of a team moving Fannie Mae out of the federal government and creating a separate company. This was July 1968. I worked on that team for about six weeks. We pulled numbers together, interviewed people and talked to all of the real estate folks to better understand their business.

At the same time, I was asked to join the team that was McKinsey's first effort for COMSAT, which was created by Congress in 1962 to serve as a public entity to develop an international satellite communication system. Although it was government regulated, COMSAT was equally owned by some major communications corporations and independent investors. They had just moved to offices in L'Enfant Plaza.

COMSAT officials had approached McKinsey because of an expertise we had developed in executive compensation. Many boards would come to us because we had one of the world's great experts in the field, Arch Patton. McKinsey was also bringing the post office out of the federal government to become a private corporation. I was part of McKinsey's growing expertise in being a bridge between the public and private sectors. They wanted me on board to use what I learned with Fannie Mae.

I soaked up a lot about consulting, especially how expensive it was for clients to bring us in. McKinsey estimated the number of hours they were going to work on a project, at what levels, and they set a price. The fees were higher than anyone else, whether it was Booz Allen or any of the other high profile consultancies. Because of their reputation and track record, McKinsey commanded these high fees.

The high fees meant several things to me. If my billing rate was, say $150 or $200 an hour, I felt under pressure to offer real solutions and not just window dressing the way some consultancies operated. I wasn't the only one who felt this pressure. We all worked our butts off to warrant the money that clients paid us. I often found myself working 10 or 12 hours on an issue and then bill for 8 hours because I felt guilty that I hadn't produced proper results for that client. I would have rather produced an end product I could be proud of instead of having the client pay for something I didn't do to my satisfaction.

The partners made a lot of money, and the unspoken promise was that you would also make a lot of money if you became a partner or director in the firm. Even as an associate, though, you put money into an ESOP program, a profit-sharing plan. From the minute you walked in the door, you were building equity with the firm.

If you were elected to be a partner, then you had to buy your partnership. This was similar to law firms because company leader Marvin Bower modeled McKinsey after law firms. He had a Harvard Law degree and a Harvard Business School degree, and took over the firm in 1933 when it was floundering. Even though the McKinsey family was no longer involved, it was a good name and Bower kept it.

McKinsey had a plethora of internal guidelines about how associates operated, even how you dressed. When I joined the firm, it was the first year that men weren't required to wear hats, but you had to wear over-the-calf socks that were black or dark blue. You had to dress in white shirts. This was all a part of the strictness and mystique of McKinsey. Working for the firm was stimulating, exciting but grueling. McKinsey's rigor, discipline and results were legendary in the world of consultancies and business usually came through word of mouth. My clients would tell other clients, and we all were expected after a year to two to begin developing a reputation with clients that would result in generating new clients.

One unique aspect of McKinsey is that we turned down clients. For example, I knew many people who were involved in building the World Trade Center. Their staff came to McKinsey and said they had a problem leasing space. They wanted our help in producing a strategy for leasing empty offices. After the meeting, I said to the head person: 'You know, it makes no sense. This is a real estate project. It doesn't have anything to do with strategy. McKinsey isn't the right firm for the job. We're not real estate people. We can't tell you what's good or bad about your property or how you go about attracting people. We could do some marketing work for you, but it would cost you three times more than a marketing firm. It would be a mistake to hire us.'

Again, I believe we were unique among consulting firms in that we regularly turned away potential clients. One of the fundamental tenets preached by McKinsey was *client, firm and self.* The client was always first. Many companies now talk about the customer, the customer, the customer, but it's often lip service. At McKinsey it was real, and if we didn't feel it was in the best interests of a client to hire us, that's what we recommended.

The client came first even before ourselves. If they wanted you there at 8 a.m. on Monday, then you were there at 8 a.m. Your family was last, and I was rarely at home. One time when I was doing a project in Philadelphia, I'd leave Alexandria on either Sunday night or first thing Monday morning and I'd be back on Friday night or Saturday morning. I would do this for weeks at a time.

On one occasion, when I was working on an out-of-town project, we finished early on Friday so I grabbed an earlier flight home. About 3 o'clock in the afternoon I was walking up the steps into our cul-de-sac. At the far end of the collection of townhouses was my daughter Christi who was about five years old. She came running and yelling: "My daddy's going to have dinner with us tonight! My daddy's going to have dinner with us," and everybody was watching. I was initially shocked, pleased with her love at seeing me. I have never forgotten the confrontation between my personal desire to be there at home and my commitment to a firm and profession that often made that impossible.

Amid this strict environment, I was learning how to handle clients, especially eccentric personalities like John Rollins, one of my first clients in the private sector. Although I had built an expertise in the public sector, I also was expected to work on several projects at the same time outside of my specialty. In the middle of my public sector work, management asked me to be the senior person working for the owners of Rollins Leasing Corporation. It was a private company with no ties to government. John Rollins' brother Wayne, who owned Rollins, Inc. had bought a company, Orkin Exterminating, before I joined McKinsey. He bought Orkin because of work that McKinsey did to help determine if it was a solid good company to buy and how he could do so. The Rollins brothers didn't have much money, but they were friends of the DuPonts, who put up the funds to buy Orkin. Two days later, they pulled in all the cash that Orkin had in its banks, gave it back to the DuPonts, and now they owned the company outright. Because of this clever deal, Wayne thought highly of McKinsey and asked us to talk to John about handling some of his deals.

John was an entrepreneur. Even though I worked with other people who would become entrepreneurs, John was a person who really had made it on his own and had done well financially. One time he spent a half day with me, discussing where the pinstripes should be located on his new Learjet. This kind of customer hand-holding was all part of working for McKinsey.

It was the age of conglomeration, and I had some expertise in this area because of the research project I had done for Monsanto about entrepreneurships existing in large corporations. The Rollins brothers were in the thick of the conglomeration movement but realized they could use McKinsey's assistance.

One time I was making a presentation to John's board, and I was standing in front of John and his brother Wayne. Even though my director agreed with my findings, I realized about half way through that I was telling them both that John, for all intents and purposes, had screwed up. I brought up some of John's decisions that were flawed; they didn't make any rational sense. I could see John's blood pressure rising.

I learned a lasting lesson here. I should have been more sensitive in how I presented my findings. Not only was John my client, paying the bills, but, more importantly, I was relating his short-comings in front of his older brother. It was my first real leader-ship role with a board and I made a rookie mistake. It was an error on my part to say these kinds of things in front of John's older brother. Certainly I owed it to my client to speak the truth, no matter how unpleasant, but the way in which I did it, in an open forum, was wrong.

There was fallout, of course. They wanted a hiatus on the study because, as they said diplomatically, 'we're trying to absorb it.' We didn't work with them until a year later. It wasn't punishment, but John clearly was unhappy with me. I said what had to be said - it was all true - but I should have done it in a considerate way. Lesson learned.

Meanwhile, COMSAT remained an ongoing project. It became a tough slog because of Chairman and CEO General Jim McCormack, a retired Air Force three-star general, whose most recent claim to fame was that he was the vice president of MIT. He had established a pack of think tanks in the Air Force and people revered him. They called him Gentleman Jim, because he always wore pinstripes and was a bit of a dandy. Unfortunately, he had a bit of trouble making executive decisions in this private sector environment. He was new to the world of business, overly cautious and used to a more collegial way of making decisions. He was the CEO, but tended to procrastinate yet he was setting a leadership mold that COMSAT was to follow for many years. Unfortunately, the senior leaders of the company came from government jobs with the exception of the CFO and we used to joke that most of them thought the term ROI (return on investment) was only a French word for king.

Just like John Rollins, COMSAT executives didn't much like what we had to say - in this case about their pay. Arch Patton, who led our compensation team, said in his first presentation to them: "You were formed by an act of Congress. The success of your venture was made when you became a monopoly for international communications…Your technology came from Hughes, so you had nothing to do with that. Your launches came from NASA. How can we possibly put in a system of bonuses that are based on measuring the performance or success of people in the organization when all of this was handed to you?

"You're asking us to recommend stock options yet you don't even properly measure executive performance. Everybody is simply expected to do whatever job it is that they're supposed to do and there isn't a solid measure of how they perform. In addition, the company makes a certain amount of profit dependent upon what the regulators give. Your shareholders are only going to benefit from the fact that you were formed and they're going to get a normal rate of return and you can't affect that in any major way. In the scheme of things, you shouldn't be getting bonuses and you shouldn't be getting stock options unless and until you are willing to establish real business objectives that have true impacts on your bottom line and you can measure performance against these."

They were angry, but they could not deny what Patton had to say because he was the "god of compensation." Nobody was better, and he was absolutely spot-on in this instance.

Not only that, but the board was a hodgepodge of personalities. It was composed of six of COMSAT'S competitors, which were from the telephone side of the house. AT&T had three seats, ITT had two and then there was an independent telephone carrier, Hawaiian Telcom. On the other side of the table were the public representatives, people like Bruce Sundlun, who was the head of the Outlet Corporation, who later became the governor of Rhode Island. There was Bill Hagerty, president of Drexel Institute of Technology, George Meany, former head of the AFL-CIO, Fred Donner, who was the chairman of the General Motors finance committee and Joseph V. Charyk, former Under Secretary of the Air Force and now COMSAT's first president. General Jim McCormack was chairman.

I would sit at the board meetings and watch as people tried to understand how to guide this new and very high-tech enterprise in a goldfish bowl, being a product of congressional action. Meany showed up for half of the meetings and said very little. Donner was at the other end and he kept mum. When one of them did say something, however, the other would respond in opposition. Not only that, the HR person was a three-martini lunch-type disaster. When Patton made his pronouncement, even the board had to eventually agree that he was right – even though they didn't like it one bit.

Nevertheless, COMSAT remained my client for the next seven years. During that time, I dealt in many efforts to adapt their organization structure and strategies to changes in that business. My work also included setting a direction for their laboratories. I never would have thought at the time that I would become the Chairman of COMSAT some 35 years later.

In the spring of '69, I started a project for Sun Oil which had bought Sunray DX and was going to merge with it. This was the largest acquisition ever seen at the time, about $900 million. Once the deal was signed, we began our work.

Our main job was to keep the companies on task and make sure, as best as we could, that their actions were honest and not politically motivated. We were in the middle of the fray, coordinating inputs from both companies to make sure that whatever occurred was in the best interests of the combined company. We established an integration taskforce, a joint McKinsey effort combining people from our Washington and New York offices. All of the laboratories and technology of Sun Oil and Sunray DX came under my purview.

The two companies were almost equal in size, but exact opposites in other ways. Sun Oil was a unique company built by J. Howard Pew and everything was gold plated. Things had to be just so. They even colored their gas with blue dye for their *Sunoco Blue* brand. In fact, one of my recommendations was to eliminate the dye, because it was costing them about $90,000 a month, and it wasn't bringing them any return. At one time, gas pumps had a little transparent window that showed the gas being pumped but that was no longer the case. You didn't see the gas being pumped anymore so the color used as a branding point was gone. It was an emotional fixation to the Pews, but we managed to convince them to eliminate the dye.

Pew was a visionary about one thing; he knew that the U.S. was too dependent upon foreign oil and we needed to find alternatives in North America. He bought a huge part of Athabasca in Canada, where tar sands were located. He was a technologist and wanted to make sure that Sun Oil took the lead on building equipment in Athabasca to mine the tar sands needed to create synthetic oil. He was dead certain that the price of oil was going up and this venture would become an alternative to foreign oil. Unfortunately, the engineering group of Sun Oil could not prove that extracting oil from tar sands was economically feasible because the price of gas was low at the time. It became part of the research department's task to prove that J. Howard was right, and they did everything they could to make it so. One of my jobs was to keep everyone honest. They kept trying to justify the Athabasca deal even going so far as to suggest that they could make money by extracting cobalt with the sand to produce natural blue glass. They thought that would be a worthwhile secondary product and researched how much blue cobalt glass the world needed. No matter how they tried to spin it, cobalt glass was a non-starter. As far as tar sands were concerned, however, Pew was insightful but ahead of his time in finding alternative sources to meet the country's energy demands.

Finally, over nine months, we merged the two companies and produced a comprehensive series of reports, which served as a blueprint for the new company. During this project, I encountered one of the more interesting leaders I have ever met. CEO Bob Dunlap was the son-in-law of one of the Pews. When he was younger, he had been picked as a junior person from the accounting office to become the president of Sun Oil, even before he married the Pew daughter. This was a long time ago, and he had been CEO for more than twenty years. While we were there, he reached down inside the organization, and identified a 35-year-old employee from the refining management organization to be his successor.

This was an even more clever move than it first appeared. For one thing, many companies felt as though the true answer to choosing a CEO was to have a fight at the upper echelon and let the victor become the top executive. This is an unpleasant process and generally leads to protracted rancor. In addition, by reaching down into the ranks, and grooming up-and-coming stars, a company sends the message that it was possible to move up in the organization. It kept those at the top sharp and provided motivation for those in middle management. It was a succession plan that offered a very different approach from others that I came across. To be sure, this was a unique management succession process, and it worked for Sun. It made me realize once again the importance of considering standard and non-standard approaches in major management decision making.

Working on the Sun Oil merger was a significant project for me. So much so that I expected to move up to partner. From that point forward, I was in charge of my own projects, running them myself, so in the back of my mind I was expecting to make partner. I was having so much fun that I didn't dwell on it, though.

I enjoyed the intensity and gratification of the work as well as bringing in my own clients.

I also handled some projects on my own that were unrelated to McKinsey. One that was particularly engaging had begun earlier in my McKinsey tenure. I had a cousin Denis who was the brother of my cousin Colin with whom I traveled through Europe while in college. He was married, in his 20s, and frustrated by his job which was working for master pewterer Englefield in London who produced the well-respected Crown & Rose line of goods, a trademark that went back hundreds of years.

We decided that we would try to establish a pewter company in Wolfeboro, New Hampshire, on Lake Winnipesauke where my sister Alice Rose lived. We would start a company and bring over Denis to be the master pewterer. If he had other people that he wanted to bring over and work with we would get them visas and do all the paperwork necessary to make sure they could legally work in the United States. Because of my chemical engineering background, I enjoyed doing the research on pewter and how it was produced. My cousin told me what kind of equipment and machinery he would need, and we purchased it. He emigrated and we set up an apartment above the shop, which was called *Hampshire Pewter.* It was a true family company because my sister, brother-in-law and I financed it. We produced pewter pieces which agents then sold. It did reasonably well until the company succumbed to the interpersonal problems that often plague family-run firms. We eventually sold the company to people who still produce pewter products.

The company failed for us because we didn't have someone leading it on a full time basis. I learned that you can't run a business, even a small one, part time. For me, personally, I realized that I didn't want to run a small business at all, especially one that involved family.

Another McKinsey project was undertaken for Pete Peterson, who was head of Bell & Howell and brought in by President Richard Nixon to be Assistant to the President for International Economic Affairs. In 1972, he became the Secretary of Commerce.

At that time he also was chairman of Nixon's National Commission on Productivity. Peterson later co-founded private equity and investment management firm, the Blackstone Group. Much later, in 2010 he signed *The Giving Pledge*, becoming one of 40 billionaires, led by Warren Buffett and Bill Gates, who agreed to give half of their wealth to charities.

While Secretary of Commerce, Peterson asked McKinsey to examine the United States' international economic capability. We were to assess the nation's competitiveness. One of our main goals was to discover what kind of information the country collected, how we used this data to make decisions and what organizations were available to carry out decisions born of this knowledge.

We performed a detailed 'deep dive' for Peterson, learning, for example, what information was collected through the census, the CIA, the Federal Reserve and other government agencies. It was extremely comprehensive. We also studied three industries - aircraft, tires and automotive - to learn what happened when the government got involved in their businesses. As part of the aircraft industry examination, we were asked to assess the SST, the Supersonic Transport, because the government was considering investing in it as were the French and British. Boeing was pushing very hard on this effort with the Nixon White House.

In the end, we responded to the Administration that the idea was a non-starter. We showed that an SST would not be economically viable any time before the turn of the century because of the expensive technologies it required. The White House people responded that the British and the French were going to build the *Concorde*, and we would be left behind. We just kept repeating our findings that both countries would end up spending a lot of money which would be wasted.

Fortunately, the White House trusted our assessment, which turned out to be correct.

Only 20 Concorde aircraft were built and it represented a substantial economic loss to France and Great Britain during its 27-year run which ended in 2003.

One of the McKinsey traits that helped us with our government work was our ability to be apolitical. The firm always had good relationships with people who were influential, whether they were bankers, lawyers, whoever they happened to be. Most of our clients happened to be Republican because most of our clients were CEOs who were more often Republican in their leanings. We would also engage in pro bono transition work for the Kennedy, Johnson and Nixon administrations as they were moving into office. We handled transition projects for six or seven different administrations on both sides of the aisle. We would most often find our way to do strategically important government work with cabinet level executives in various administrations because they were the only officials with the ability to do sole source procurement. We could never easily compete for broad-base procurements, because we were too expensive. A secretary's office actually had to put themselves on the line and say, "we need McKinsey."

Another project I was proud of was, in fact, a pro bono job for the World Wildlife Fund, an organization established to protect endangered species, which was why their symbol was a panda bear. Prince Bernhard of the Netherlands and Prince Philip of the U.K. were co-heads and early sponsors. It was a European group, but when I got involved in '73 they had formed a U.S. counterpart headed by Roy Chapin who was chairman of American Motors. The board was composed of biologists, financial people and others including Arthur Godfrey and Charles Lindbergh. Lindbergh was special to me because my original grammar school in Kenmore, New York was named for the aviator. It was also an interesting sign of the times that the president of the WWF was also president of the National Rifle Association.

McKinsey was brought in to help the group restructure so they could operate more efficiently.

One time Godfrey showed up for a meeting in New York. I believe he flew his own plane into Teterboro. He was intensely interested in the WWF activities and added his celebrity weight to their effort. Interestingly enough, about ten years later, his son-in-law Bob Schmidt became involved in the telecom business and a friend. Another person on the WWF board was John Murchison, a Texas oilman and entrepreneur who was one of the Fund's benefactors. Although I didn't know it then, he and his brother Clint would play important roles in my business life later on.

It was around this time, in the summer of 1976, that I reached a defining moment at McKinsey. I had been there for eight years, and partner elections were coming up. I thought that I finally would be elected. After all, I had done good work, toiled hard and tirelessly and brought in clients.

In the early part of my career at the firm, John Garrity was my mentor. He was an extremely bright HBS graduate from a first-generation Irish family who called Worcester, Massachusetts their home. John was aggressive yet funny and wasn't uptight about many things. He was a strong leader for the Washington office and very much a part of the politics of the firm. But the reason he was running the Washington office was that nobody else in a leadership position in the firm wanted to spend much time on government issues. He was outspoken, and he could be arrogant. He didn't connect too terribly well with our business clients but did very well with our government clients. He didn't have a large cheering section at the firm, but he was astute and clever enough to have the right friends who wanted him to stay.

I was unique at McKinsey in that partnership elections were expected in four or five years and I had been right on that edge more times than most. Indeed, I stayed on because I was encouraged to do so each time I was thinking of leaving, but after eight years it appeared that either our office, John's internal political support, or my overall performance as compared to other candidates failed to meet the test for my electability.

I knew that if I didn't make partner this time my days were pretty well numbered. The firm would not overtly ask me to leave because I was an asset, but when you got turned down for partner the attitude toward you changed in subtle ways.

It was now or never to make partner and unfortunately it was never. Some might say I was loyal to a fault for staying so long but I disagree. I was doing what I loved, and yes, a sense of loyalty is one of my strands.

And it paid off.

I decided that it was time to move on when David Hertz, one of the directors from McKinsey's New York office, called. "Brian," he said, "I really need you to do something for me. Pan Am has been one of my big clients. Bill Seawell, who runs the company, is on the board of an organization and they're trying to gain some traction." Seawell was an Air Force general and his job before Pan Am was as commandant of cadets at the Air Force Academy. "A classmate of his, General George Brown who is now the chairman of the Joint Chiefs, along with the former Secretary of State, Dean Rusk, and the publisher of the *Denver Post*, Donald Seawell (no relation to Bill Seawell) and Bill want to start an institute and they need someone like you to give it hands-on management to get it established."

David was one of my proponents at McKinsey, and I liked him very much. "Brian, I know that you've come to the conclusion that you can no longer work at McKinsey, but I would like you to stay with the firm long enough to do this project for me. We'll give you a leave of absence and you can use the project as a vehicle to help you move on to whatever you want to do next."

The idea was intriguing: an institute that would bring together the brain trusts of the civilian and military sectors so they could better understand each other. The Vietnam War had driven a wedge between the two groups, and the goal of the newly-forming Civilian Military Institute was to build a bridge between both sides to help cut through some of the divisiveness and animosity that was prevalent in the country. CMI was to identify the issues separating the groups and start a dialogue.

The organization was to be located in Colorado Springs through support from the Air Force Academy because of General Brown. They had raised some funds, hired staff and were ready to begin work. Bill Seawell felt strongly about the Institute because

68

he believed the military was getting a bad rap over the Vietnam War and the anger building in many Americans about the military. I flew to New York and met with Bill Seawell and it was clear to me after we spoke for several hours that this project was important to him. 'I know that you're interested and you're involved,' I said. 'I would like to meet with Dean Rusk and General Brown, listen to what they have to say. I want to gauge their commitment before I decide to do this.'

Within twenty-four hours I met with Rusk who was now head of the law school at the University of Georgia. I spent the entire day with him. The following day, Thursday, I met with General Brown at the Pentagon. I sat in the offices of the chairman of the Joint Chiefs and we talked for three hours. When I left he said: "I hope you will consider helping us."

No sooner did I return home than I came down with the flu. I was lying in bed on Saturday morning feeling miserable when Mary Ann said there was a phone call. She said, "Brian, there's a phone call for you from the Pentagon. It's General Brown."

"Brian," he said, "I felt I had to call you, because you lied to me." Good lord. What did I do wrong? 'What do you mean, General?' He said: "Well, I've got your resume here, and it says that you're 195 pounds. And it's my guess that you haven't been 195 pounds for years." It wasn't an insult but his somewhat awkward way of starting a conversation. "Really," he said, "I'm calling to encourage you to take on the project." This was the start of a unique and close friendship I developed with George Brown.

I couldn't say 'no.' Before I knew it, I had an office at the Pan Am offices in Washington and another one in Colorado Springs. I became executive director of the Civilian Military Institute and began to construct their organizational structure. I decided to take the organization through a conference and produce a document for posterity.

We were able to put on a three-day symposium with many influential people attending and offering presentations. We had people like Bill Colby, head of the CIA. On the civilian side, we had

Peter Krogh, who later became head of the Georgetown School for International Studies. He had been a White House fellow for Dean Rusk when he was Secretary of State. We also had George Kennan, perhaps the greatest living Western expert on Russia and the Soviet Union. We got Admiral Duke Bain, who was head of the National Defense University and General Andrew Goodpaster, who had commanded NATO and became superintendent of West Point to help guide them after the school's cheating scandal.

I convinced John Dunlop, who was Secretary of Labor under Nixon and now a professor at Harvard's Kennedy School of Government, to be co-host of the event along with David Packard of Hewlett-Packard.

We hosted people from all sides, and I knew that we had done a fair and impartial job when I was sitting in the offices of Pan Am and came across a column that Jack Anderson wrote disparaging the CMI as yet another part of the military-industrial complex. On the same day I received a letter from the American Strategic Institute - an organization that was a little to the right of the Attila the Hun - saying that the Civilian Military Institute was a pinko-commie operation. I knew then that I had done a solid job - right down the political middle.

The whole project took seven months. It included a seminal three-day meeting in Colorado Springs which examined the most difficult aspects of the post World War II era. When we were done, we published the proceedings in a book titled *Building a Durable Peace.*

I wish I could say that the effort turned out to be a vehicle propelling me to my next position, but it didn't work out that way. Instead, I received a phone call around the time of the symposium from David Williams who I had met at my friend's wedding and with whom I had kept in touch during my stint at McKinsey. David and his cousins John and Charles – who were brothers – restarted the Williams Brothers Company in Tulsa, Oklahoma, after World War II. The original pipeline company was established in 1910 by other family members, but John, Charles and David were raised by David's mother and father along with Joe, David's younger brother. They all attended Yale. The new entity called Williams Brothers Corp. was led by John; Charles was the outside person and David was the engineer. During the 1950s and '60s, it was the world's largest pipeline builder. Joe had joined the trio in the 1960s but by the early '70s the oil business had hit the skids, and they were casting about for something else to do.

When David heard that I was leaving McKinsey he asked if I would meet with him in Oklahoma. "I want you to come out," David said. "We've spun off a company out of Williams Brothers Corporation which we call Williams Brothers Engineering and Resource Sciences, and we put them together into a group called Resource Sciences Corporation."

He knew from our discussions that I enjoyed dealing with conglomerates, and that I had an expertise in chemical process engineering.

David continued: "We need someone to be a strategist, do our planning. We're running pretty well. We're making a lot of money. We're one of the largest engineering firms in the country and our main business is building pipelines and doing major projects all over the world. We need somebody who's able to help me to sit back and look at our business and say, 'Are we going in the right direction? Where should we go?'"

They had already combined Resource Sciences with several other companies owned by Earl Slick and then bought U.S. Filter, a small petroleum catalyst company in California. They did a reverse merger with a small company so they were able to call the new company U.S. Filter, listed on the AMEX. The new company was headed by Ray Rich.

David and Morgan Greenwood, the president, made me an offer, so Mary Ann and I flew to Tulsa to look at housing and see whether we would like the area. I hadn't yet accepted the offer, and I actually had another one in the wings, so we were talking about our next move.

Just about that time, March 1977, Bill Seawell called me. "We're having an inaugural flight of the Boeing 747 SP. We're going to

Sydney, Australia, and I wondered if you and Mary Ann would like to go on the first flight, just as a thank-you for what you did for us."

The author and wife Mary Ann celebrated the wedding of their son Brandon; May 1997.
Author's collection.

That sounded like fun, so when we returned home from Oklahoma we had the opportunity to travel on the plane's maiden voyage, a 16-hour flight from Los Angeles. We were somewhere over the Pacific, talking about the house we had seen in Tulsa and whether we wanted to move at all. Mary Ann was wary of the move because it meant picking up everything we had and selling our house in Annandale, Virginia, which we had bought in the fall of 1969. My son Brandon was born three days after we had moved into the house that September.

The McKinsey era was now over for me, and I had taken away lessons that would serve me well. I know it's a cliché, but one of the things I learned at McKinsey was that CEOs put their pants on one leg at a time, and a lot of them aren't necessarily smarter than anyone else. McKinsey gave you the opportunity to assess how these leaders got their positions. Was it that they were the most brash or the most egotistical, or did they really have leadership skills?

I learned that having the brains didn't necessarily make you the right guy, and having the style didn't necessarily make you the right guy either. I fully believed that power and position were earned by doing the right things every day. There were exceptions of course, and sometimes bad actors rose to the top but they were the outliers.

The other thing that I came away with was an understanding of how companies should be organized. Clients were often concerned that they weren't organized correctly; they wanted us to tell them how to reorganize. A massive McKinsey study on the subject concluded that there was no right way to organize. You can organize geographically. You can organize by product. You can organize by function. It didn't matter. The right organization depended upon the people in the company. People determined whether a company was organized efficiently or not. The corollary of this is that companies should build an organization around the people who are going to run it. They're the ones calling the shots. Unfortunately, you don't always know how these people will perform if they've never been in a similar position. You had to know the people who worked for you and trust them. For a McKinsey associate it wasn't easy to determine how well a person would perform because we weren't around long enough to know their strengths and weakness. We could only guess and that was the best that we could do. Fortunately for me, after nine years at McKinsey, I became pretty good at guessing.

I was proud of the work I had done at McKinsey but now it was time to move on. Mary Ann and I both decided that relocating to Tulsa was the right step for us. We pulled up roots and moved to Oklahoma where I became the senior vice president for planning and marketing for Resource Sciences Corporation in June 1977.

When I joined RSC they had projects all over the world, including a gas pipeline being built from southern Iran to Russia. They also were trying to build a pipeline from the McKenzie Delta in Canada to carry gas to the United States. They were engaged in the biggest pipeline project at the time, which was the Sohio pipeline designed to carry all of the Alaskan crude from Long Beach, California, to Midlands, Texas. We were planning to reverse the usual flow on a 48-inch gas pipeline with the goal of carrying two million barrels a day, which was coming out of Alaska. The whole idea was to avoid having to take all the Alaskan crude and ship it through the Panama Canal.

Another project was a contract with the Navy to run the Elk Hills oil reserve. The heavy crude was used to create a source of bunker fuel for Navy shipping needs. The company also managed the structural engineering firm Holmes & Narver in California which was involved in projects in Saudi Arabia.

My job was to make sure that all of these projects and plans fit together, made sense and were profitable. I worked with David to make sure we were planning for the future. Because the oil business is cyclical, one of the challenges was to plan for the down times and capitalize on the high times, but especially to make sure we got through the low cycles to fight another day.

We had many large projects, but one that was particularly ambitious – although it didn't go forward – was with the government of Saudi Arabia to build an actual city. Because of threats from Iran and elsewhere, the Saudi government wanted a city that could be defended against attack. They were also planning to build a factory to produce rockets, mortars and other armaments to protect the Arab states. The government had some contractors ready to go, including Edward Durell Stone, the architect who had designed the U.S. Pavilion at the World's Fair in Brussels, which, incidentally, I had visited during my trip to Europe with my cousin. The city would be located 90 miles south of Riyadh and cost about $20 billion.

The Saudis put out a Request for Proposal and construction companies across the world wanted a piece of it, including us. I was the person chosen from headquarters to try and secure the business. We decided to combine forces with European construction companies, because U.S. construction companies shied away from the job. Many felt they couldn't do business in that part of the world without payoffs, and they were loathe to do that because of U.S. laws. European companies ... well, we didn't ask them how they got entry to the business. We signed arrangements with two of the largest European construction companies – Bilfinger Berger in Germany and Siab, a Scandinavian company. Our partner was Modern Arab Construction. The plan was for us to be the main engineers for the construction.

My charge was to represent Williams Brothers. We had meetings all over the world, and I spent a lot of time and effort bringing the entire proposal together. About halfway through the process, the Saudi Ministry of Defense made it clear to everybody that it would be a single-source contract and one of their requirements designed to weed out insincere bidders was to demand a five percent bond with the bid. Five percent of $20 billion was $1 billion and a huge chunk of money. How could you risk a billion dollars? Nobody had ever done that before and it was a huge stumbling block.

The request was clearly unreasonable and had come from an Air Force lieutenant and royal family member, Prince Bandar, who later became ambassador to the United States. He was the family's lead on the project. He was young and somewhat inexperienced and made these sorts of outrageous pronouncements. There was always talk of money going under the table. Finally, the project died of its own weight.

During the two years I was there, it had become clearer to me every day that this particular business owed much of its successes and failures to serendipity and the economy – factors over which we had no control. No matter how much you planned and strategized the vagaries of the economic landscape often determined your future. This kind of company was not for me.

One sad aspect of leaving Resource Sciences was that we enjoyed Tulsa. Mary Ann and I realized that it was one of our favorite places to live. We felt bad about the need to move our children twice in two years and the possible negative impact that might have on their lives.

In fact, my next job would be in Ann Arbor, Michigan, and would turn out to be a disaster.

Chapter 7

"Brian, We've Got A Problem. The Mice Have All Died."

While still working at McKinsey, I met George Pantos who was on Pete Peterson's staff at the White House. We became friends over the years and always kept in touch. George was on the board of Gelman Sciences, a company that produced membranes used for microfiltration. They were heavily involved in applications for the pharmaceutical business. At the time, there were only two companies in the country engaged in this specialty: Gelman and Pall Corporation.

George had told me that the board was upset with the CEO and founder Charlie Gelman because he couldn't seem to manage the company properly. They wanted someone else to take over the reins.

I wanted to try my hand at running a company so I visited Ann Arbor and my first impression of Gelman was its small size, only about a hundred or so people. Even though I wanted to work in a larger company, I thought I could be happy there. The plan was for the board to ease out the CEO while I took charge of the operation.

It turned out to be a dumb move for me.

I was counting on the board to do what they promised, slowly move out the CEO while I ran the company. If I had done my homework, I would have realized that the same board had been around for about 15 years and had gone through cycles of liking and disliking the CEO's performance. What I thought was the final straw with the CEO was just another cycle. I also didn't take into account that the CEO was also the founder and knew where all the bones were buried.

I was a bit naïve about how some small companies operated. I later asked one of my former colleagues at McKinsey who told me that this kind of dance between the CEO and board is common at many small companies. Ninety-nine percent of the time this happens exactly the same way, that it was predictable. There were a few people on the board who really wanted to change leadership, but the rest of them were content with the status quo. As a result, nothing ever changed.

Of course, I didn't know any of this when we moved to Michigan. Ann Arbor was supposed to be a vibrant college town, a cultural center, but we didn't like living there especially when we arrived in March to see ice on the ground and gray skies. Mary Ann hadn't wanted to move there, but she acquiesced. Compared to Tulsa, which we loved, Ann Arbor was atrocious.

To make matters worse, we had leased a house from a Ford Motors executive who was assigned to the Far East. The house hadn't been lived in for a while and between the time that we signed the lease and packed our furniture and possessions, one of the other real estate agents in the firm - without *our* real estate agent knowing it - had given a short-term lease to a group of youngsters who stayed beyond their time period. They were squatting. We showed up and the house was filled with people, smoking dope and tearing the house apart. Under Michigan law we couldn't just throw them out, so we had to engage in a legal battle while we lived in a hotel. It was an ugly situation, a bad start that got progressively worse.

I hadn't yet figured out that I wouldn't receive backing from the board, so I began to meet with people, planned to restructure the company, do what I thought I was hired to do. While I was trying to understand the company's politics, people were coming to me and relating terrible stories about what was going on.

One story that horrified me was about the head of engineering, who had been with the company about eight years although he was not there when I joined the company. Charlie was driving him mercilessly to finish a product because the sales people were already selling it to customers. The engineer was being hounded around the clock and finally died of a heart attack after three weeks of constant work and pressure from above. At the funeral, the engineer's wife openly blamed Charlie for her husband's death - in front of everyone - but Charlie simply shrugged off her accusations.

Things got even worse.

I met with the vice president of manufacturing, and it turned out that he previously had been in charge of keeping the plant clean as head of maintenance. He had successfully and rapidly moved up the company ranks, but he didn't have much of a clue about manufacturing. I went to Charlie and said that I wanted to fire this fellow, but Charlie refused to back me. That was another indication that things were not exactly kosher at the company considering that I was executive VP and responsible specifically for operations, a position that didn't exist before I got there. It should have been within my purview to fire this obviously incompetent person, but I relented and told Charlie that I would try to coach him, which I did for over a week without much success.

Then, somebody from engineering and process control came to me and said: "Brian, we've got a problem. The mice have all died."

'The what? The mice?' I had no idea what he was talking about. 'What does that mean?'

"Brian, for the last eight months we have been manufacturing a line of filtration products, testing them in the labs, and the test mice died. This means the filters are toxic, and when we found out they were poisonous we went to Charlie, who said, "It's the customer's responsibility to test the products they receive. We will continue shipping until they tell us otherwise."

I confronted Charlie with the evidence. Pointing to the test sheets, I said: 'It says here that it's toxic.'

He replied: "It says nothing to that effect."

I was livid. 'Toxic products are going to pharmaceutical companies. I'm not going to be connected with this.'

That was the end of my three-month career at Gelman.

I also had learned why I couldn't fire the vice-president of manufacturing. He apparently had a much closer personal relationship with Charlie than anyone could or should have expected. In addition, I also discovered that the person I hired to be *my* assistant learned that Charlie's assistant had been going through my trash can. My assistant was fired for alerting me. The place was nuts.

We were still stuck with a big house in a city we didn't like. My daughter was having a rough time in school because of the turmoil of the 1970s. Mary Ann was still unhappy with Ann Arbor compared to Tulsa, which we both adored. Luckily, my son was happy playing softball and having a good time. I felt badly that I had brought my family to Michigan and I didn't know what to do next. Fortunately, the board agreed to severance and healthcare coverage for two months, so there was some wiggle room to figure it out.

I spent the summer thinking about my next position, taking my time to make sure that I got it right this time. I was still upset with myself that I hadn't checked out Gelman more fully. It was another rookie mistake.

Through a colleague at McKinsey, I learned that Clint Murchison was starting up a new business called Subscription Television of America. Even though he was based in Dallas, Clint started the company in Washington, DC, to be close to the Federal Communications Commission. This was important to the company's success because pay television was a new idea and much of their success would depend upon FCC rulemakings. This was 1979, and pay TV was just starting as was HBO, which had begun its first cable service in San Diego.

Clint had purchased decoder technology from a Canadian company called Electrohome that could encode a television signal and then decode it in a box on your television set. A broadcaster could use that box to sell motion pictures to home viewers. Our plan was to negotiate with producers and distributors allowing us to rebroadcast movies just after they left movie theaters but before they made it to over-the-air, free television. The concept was revolutionary, but others had also figured out that this could be the next wave including HBO which was then part of Time Warner. They also were trying to bring movies to the nascent cable business for an add-on price.

Our system broadcast over the underutilized UHF over-the-air TV channels. These were channels 14 and up. UHF had never gotten any traction because of competition from the networks which had the VHF channels locked up. No matter what they did, the FCC had little success populating the UHF channels with content providers, so they were looking at alternatives for the unused channels and pay TV was one idea.

I was brought in to deal with the regulators, the FCC, and anyone else I needed to negotiate with to get this idea going. I also had to deal with Clint, which wasn't easy. His brother John, who was really the brains behind their businesses, died a year earlier. As somebody once described Clint, "He could get lost in a crowd of two." His father had given him 50 million dollars when he was 21 and said, "Go and build something," so he and John built their empire. Now he was reputed to be worth 400 million dollars. Unfortunately, he didn't meet a deal he wouldn't do and was flying high because he and his brother had built up all of these companies. Once John died, under Texas law, they had to unwind the partnership, but the problem was that the many children affected by their estates were not on the same page at all. Clint's own children had become distant from him as well because he had divorced their mother and married a woman for whom they didn't much care. John's kids didn't like Clint either, but mainly because their father John was now gone, and they felt that Clint didn't know how to run the business. They were convinced that John was the brains behind the operation, and Clint had made some bad business calls. He did make some good ones, though, like founding the Dallas Cowboys in 1960.

I know this sounds funny to say, but dealing with Texans at the time took some getting used to. They handled things differently in the Lone Star State during the oil boom days. For example, the big question in many partnership deals was "who's the screwee and who's the screwer." The phrase I heard was: "If you borrow from a friend, that's profit; if you have to pay him back, that's loss." It was called the "First Texas Law of Business." Unfortunately for Clint, he was too often the screwee. He was forever being hustled. He relied on his law firm, Jenkins and Gilchrist, a highly reputable firm, to keep him from getting caught up in the next scam. Their job was to keep him clean and out of jail.

I remember one of Clint's boyhood friends, who was Clint's partner in some Libyan deals, purloined seven million dollars from him. Clint gave him money to start up a project and he simply sent it to a Swiss bank account. We tracked him down, told Clint, and he said, "I'll take care of it." His way of taking care of it was to banish the guy from being on the floor at the Dallas Cowboys football game. Clint had bought the NFL franchise in 1960 and decreed that this guy could no longer sit by the bench. That was all he did to the man who stole millions from him.

There were a lot of other weird goings-on, too. One time I wasn't getting paid and after a particularly long discussion, I got a check from the Cowboys account - we called it *Clint's Begging Bowl* because they were the only ones with cash - and each of his failing ventures could often be kept running with loans from the Cowboys.

Clint had started the subscription TV business in San Francisco with two friends from Dallas. The first was W.O. Bankston, a big SMU benefactor and successful car dealer. Bankston was well liked and played the role of father confessor and confidant to many of the Dallas Cowboys players. Everyone loved W.O. because of his wonderful attitude and positive ways. As an example, he would buy 400 Super Bowl tickets for friends and acquaintances no matter where the game took place. He also would buy 400 tickets to the Texas/Oklahoma football game in Dallas and his friends would come and party. He owned a large Lincoln Mercury Ford dealership. One of his claims to fame was that he knew Babe Ruth. The other partner was Max Williams, a wealthy oil field type and former state tennis champion, who was, like the rest of the oilmen, very aggressive and levered up to the hilt.

The San Francisco station license was owned by Lillian Lincoln Howell of the Lincoln Electric family from Cleveland. She was broadcasting Chinese language programming during the day and wanted us to program movies at night. She needed our money to keep the station from going bankrupt. She was an incredibly odd recluse who drove around in an armored Ford van and was always sure somebody was going to blow her up or otherwise dispatch her. She had a house in Hillsboro across the street from Bing Crosby's old house. Her own house had once been magnificent, like a miniature Versailles, but nobody had done any upkeep for 20 years. You could see huge pieces of art on the wall, masterpieces, but they were dirty, dusty and some had holes and rips in the canvases. The drapes were half hanging and half not. The swimming pool was covered with algae. She also had a son who walked around with a stove pipe hat and beard apparently because his first name was Lincoln.

We had a strong business plan, and the idea was to reach a breakeven level of subscribership first and then begin to make money. We began building the company, and there were five other stations around the country doing the same thing. We wrestled against a time crunch because the FCC required that you start broadcasting within a specified time period, so we had to move quickly.

One of our strategies was to establish an association of the new operators, not only to represent ourselves before the FCC but to work with suppliers and others because we had common interests. We were not competitors because we were located in different cities. This association, which at one point represented operators in 30 major cities, would help in negotiating with studios such as Fox and Warner Brothers to broadcast certain films. We offered a monthly menu of films which were shown and re-shown at various times. Subscribers paid a set fee to watch all of the movies on the menu.

It was not pay-per-view; that technology did not exist. There was one company that tried to do pay-per-view, but the technology was too complex, sent through the telephone system, and it really didn't work well. On one occasion, in fact, the telephone system in Los Angeles was brought to its knees in 1979 during a planned showing of *The Deep*.

Our idea was simpler than that. Each decoder box would allow you to watch the channel as we broadcast movies live. Our main problem was piracy. It didn't take a genius to bust the system. So as quickly as we put these decoders out there, people could buy equipment to watch for free.

The other problem was that we had no money, so we had to create everything off the cuff. At the same time, though, everyone thought we had plenty of money because we were being backed by supposedly rich Texans. Sadly, Clint was very sick with an illness akin to Lou Gehrig's disease. His health was going fast, and he had reached the point that when people met him they thought he was drunk because he was slurring his speech. Before we knew it, he wasn't coming to meetings and the company was three months behind in my salary. On top of that, they owed their lawyers over a million dollars.

If that wasn't enough, we had bought a station in Providence, Rhode Island. The state had only three VHF stations and one UHF station which actually was located in Rehoboth, Massachusetts. The Providence station was established in 1953 when UHF station licenses were just being issued. During my search to find possible stations for our service, this one barely hit the radar screen because not all of the public domain paperwork was available. Once I learned that this station had been dark for 24 years while everyone else without an operating station had their licenses revoked, I could not understand why. Subsequently, I learned that the license was owned by a judge named Arcaro who happened to be Rhode Island Senator John Pastore's former law partner. Pastore was head of the Senate Communications Subcommittee and was best known for taking part in the first hearings to fund the Public Broadcasting System. Somehow the station kept getting extensions to its license even though it wasn't broadcasting. It was even odder than that. The call sign was WNET, which was in use by the public television in New York City on channel 13. Moreover, this station which piqued our interest was on channel 14, which was no longer in use by UHF stations.

According to FCC rules, a license owner could not make a profit on selling a station or a station license unless it was in operation. This was to prevent people from obtaining licenses and flipping them, a term called *trafficking*. You could, however, recover the money you invested in the license. I went to the owner and said, 'I understand that to buy something like this would cost two or three million bucks if it was operating. Maybe five million. We can't offer you any more than what you have already sunk into it. I'm willing to pay you $400,000.' He took it.

We had this valuable license but no money to build a station. In fact, we had bought other licenses, one in Chicago, one in Dallas and even one my own backyard, Washington, DC, which was Channel 50. Our partner for Channel 50 was Jack Kent Cooke, who owned the Washington Redskins football team. The money for Channel 50 came from Cooke, who had bought Teleprompter out of bankruptcy after the owner went to prison for bribing the Harrisburg city council. Teleprompter equipment was used for racetrack wagering. Cooke owned the majority interest in the station and during a Monday night football game between the Redskins and the Giants, I got Clint together with Cooke and we bought the rights to broadcast pay TV on Channel 50. We had also negotiated some cash flow from Teleprompter to help cover our costs.

All during this period, I was still trying to raise funding to build our stations while dealing with Clint and his odd deals. For instance, someone talked Clint into buying a company called CRAP which should have told me something about its prospects from the start. The name was short for the *Calorific Recovery Anaerobic Process*, a process developed to recover methane from cow manure.

The idea was to buy access to the feed lots of cattle producers. When the cows were in their feed lots before they were slaughtered they would be in a facility where the manure would drop through to a collector. You quickly took that manure and put it into another facility where it would get very hot and produce methane. You would then suck out the methane, compress it and send it out through gas pipelines to consumers. I was trying to raise money for my TV stations at the same time that Clint's other people were trying to raise money for CRAP. Clint also had an events exhibition company in Houston, and another company, Corland Corporation, that built shopping centers in Long Island and he owned the Las Palmas resort in Puerto Rico. There seemed to be no end to his deals, but so many needed cash at a time when all his assets were frozen or tied up.

All of this was going on at the same time. Finally, after two years, I decided that I had enough of this craziness. Almost every night I would say to Mary Ann: 'You're not going to believe this; you can't imagine what's going on here.' I was feeling a mixture of 'what did I get myself into,' along with 'this is really funny.' I didn't know whether to laugh or cry at the nonsense around me.

Finally, I was done with the subscription TV business.

I left in 1981, but about two years earlier, around the time I took the job with STV, I had met a man with the unlikely name of V. Orville Wright - no relation to the early aviator. We had talked about me working for his company called MCI where he was president. They were trying to figure out how to build their microwave network beyond a link from St. Louis to Chicago. They were going to turn it into a private line telephone service, but they were also considering going into the residential telephone business, which they were not authorized to do. They wanted me to be the head of planning, which I really didn't want to do because I had just done it at Resource Sciences.

Sometimes in life, however, you get a second chance. And when I left STV, I talked to Orville again. Now was the right time for me to work at MCI.

Chapter 8

'Ready, Fire!' There Was No Time For 'Aim' At MCI

I was eager to work at MCI, but a tad hesitant considering the last several companies with which I was involved. Orville and I negotiated for several months before we came to an agreement. The sticking point was that he wanted me to be head of planning, and I wanted an 'action' job. We settled on a title of *Senior Vice President of Corporate Development*, and I joined MCI in September 1981.

It was an exciting proposition. Not only was MCI altering the face of telecommunications - changing it from a de facto monopoly business dominated by AT&T into an unregulated business on the long distance side - but it struck me that they could actually make payroll.

I thought this would be a refreshing change, although I later found out that only a few months earlier they nearly *couldn't* make payroll.

I met with the senior staff and liked all of them. There were seven, and I made the eighth. My only trepidation was that they wanted me to be a 'thinker' instead of a 'doer.' At many companies, the new discipline called corporate development is not taken seriously, but I was sure that Bill McGowan, the chairman and CEO, was sincere when he said to me: "I want the others in the senior staff to keep their eyes on the business at hand and try to get things done right now. But I need someone to poke their head above water and look around, see where we should be going, and then help move us in that direction." That would be me.

The other members of the senior management team who would help Bill and Orville move this company into the telecom "hall of fame" included John Worthington, Sr. VP and General Counsel. He had introduced Bill to the founder of MCI, Jack Goeken, who had convinced Bill to invest and take it over. Ken Cox, a former FCC commissioner had joined as Sr. VP Regulatory and was truly MCI's "Mr. Clean," keeping the public and regulatory image of MCI where it needed to be. Bert Roberts was Sr. VP Operations, building the switching systems and customer interfaces, and Tom Leming was Sr. VP Transmission Systems and was building the MCI nationwide network. Wayne English was Sr. VP Finance and CFO and had joined MCI from TWA. Carl VorderBrugge, a long-time IBMer, was Sr. VP Sales and Marketing, and finally, Charlie Skibo was Sr. VP Planning and Administration who joined from Exxon. This team would create the foundation that made MCI the vibrant, vital company it would be throughout the 1980s.

I appreciated Bill from the minute I met him. There was an immediate kinship. We were both HBS graduates from Irish, blue collar families and both chemical engineers. His father worked for the railroad, and, like my father, was involved in union activities. Bill and I had worked for some pretty crazy outfits, too.

The first thing I did - once I got a good sense of what the company was about – was to sit back and think through what we should be doing. This was Bill's charge to me. So, once I found my way around and hired an assistant, I was ready to start. Instead, however, I found myself enmeshed in a sensitive personnel issue.

MCI had already started their residential business in Denver earlier that year. Bill's executive assistant, Jerry Taylor, had been in charge of the project. Bill had hired Jerry as the fifth or sixth employee of the company back in '68, and now, 13 years later, he still considered Jerry his executive assistant, doing all the odd jobs that he wanted him to do. Jerry was a young guy who wasn't getting much respect in the company; Bill really cared for and appreciated him but apparently never told him. Jerry had received a job offer from Western Union and he told Bill that he was going to leave MCI.

"Save him," Bill implored me. "See what you can do to keep Jerry."

The next day Jerry and I talked for almost three hours. I said, 'Look, Jerry, I don't know where the hell this thing's going because I'm new to the company. You've been here so long that you'd be a great asset to me if you would join me. And not only that, I think we're going to be doing some exciting projects. I heard from Bill that you were going with this telex company, but do you really want to do that? I think we've got a huge opportunity here.' I told him about my interest in the new cellular phone business that was just getting started. I said it was something that we should be thinking about. Beyond that, I told him that there was going to be a future in the data business, and a lot of other firms were getting involved in that, too.

I was able to keep Jerry at MCI, and he became my first vice president for corporate development. I wasn't able to offer him much more money - I know he was offered more at Western Union - but I could offer him stock options. I had done Bill a big favor not only by keeping Jerry but also saving him from political embarrassment if Jerry had jumped ship.

One senior person in the company had seen me take on Jerry and thought he could unload some undesirable people on me as well, but I wasn't biting. One of his part-time planning staff woke up in the morning and found his wife dead in bed next to him and he didn't remember what had happened. For all I knew, he got drunk, blacked out and killed her. His boss, another senior vice president, thought that because I was new that I might be an easy way out of his personnel problem. Thanks, but no thanks.

The first organizing structure that I developed was very brief but turned out to be seminal to the company. I invited Bill and

Orville to my office, and I drew on a flipchart. I began, 'The one thing I've learned in my consulting career is that if we're going be dealing with top management issues in any company, you've got to bring it down to the basics. If you do anything on a matrix that's more than two-by-two it gets confusing.'

I drew a box. 'Here it is. It's four quadrants. Voice and data. Domestic and international.'

Voice	Data
Domestic	International

At the time, I considered giving it another dimension by separating *wireline* service from *wireless* but I decided against it. I wanted to keep things simple.

No matter which two you mixed in the matrix, it was a business in which I thought MCI should be involved. They liked the idea. I think the simplicity and logic of it appealed to them. I pointed out that MCI currently was residing in just one small area of the matrix which straddled the voice and domestic boxes. They both asked me to put some meat on the bones, fill in the matrix and I did. This fundamental concept became the basis of everything MCI did from then on.

I learned that Xerox had played the 'white knight' when it bought Western Union International, but it appeared that WUI wouldn't fit anymore with an announced change in Xerox's strategy. WUI was a data transmission company that had relationships with telephone companies and government agencies all over the world, mainly for its telex service. WUI was supposed to dovetail with Xerox's XTEN project, an ambitious data transmission system that stood for Xerox Telecommunications Network that would circumvent local phone companies by using microwave antennas placed atop strategically-located buildings. This arrangement would bypass local phone lines which were not capable of handling higher speed data compared to XTEN. Xerox had hoped to establish a national network using satellites and interconnect with WUI to send and receive data globally. XTEN was ahead of its time but too costly. To make matters worse, Xerox also was under attack from Japanese copier firms.

Xerox decided to call it quits. They no longer had any use for WUI, but MCI did. It would help us get into the international data business - two boxes of the matrix. Mainly, I believed that it would give us a way of 'cracking' the international voice monopoly that AT&T enjoyed by virtue of its relationships outside of the United States.

I also learned, after doing some homework, that the person being named CEO at Xerox was David Kerns, who Orville knew from his days at IBM. This might offer us entrée.

'Bill, here's an opportunity for us to get in the international business,' I told McGowan. 'Xerox wants to get rid of WUI because they just announced that they're getting out of the XTEN project. Apparently, they haven't yet decided what to do with it.' He summoned Orville and asked him to call his contact at Xerox. As usual, the response was 'not for sale;' that's what companies usually say to such a cold call. They needed some time to think about what they were going to do.

About two weeks later, their representatives at Goldman Sachs called us and asked if we were interested. I put together a team of about ten people to go after the acquisition, and we captured the first meeting they had with perspective buyers. We told them how serious we were about buying WUI, but their bankers kept telling us that we were too small a company to come up with the money.

After some back and forth, we agreed to buy the dying telex company for $185 million. Many of our internal people said it was the worst thing we could do. These naysayers thought that we were buying a fading business – telex – which would disappear once higher-speed data methods came along, which they certainly would. They also contended that the paging business (WUI also owned Airsignal, a paging company that had domestic wireless carrier licenses in over 40 cities) would give way to mobile phone expansion.

Nate Kantor, President of MCI's Northeast Division (left), and the author refereed team-building games during an offsite meeting at Lake George, New York; June 1986.
Author's collection.

What they and outside speculators didn't realize is that WUI gave us a way to not only enter the international voice and data business, but the newly-developing cellular phone business as well, because under FCC rules we could use Airsignal's paging businesses as a local presence if we filed for cellular licenses in those markets.

At the time, most foreign governments owned their country's telecommunications networks. In order to interconnect our network to theirs - allowing our customers to talk overseas - we would have to negotiate contracts with each individual country. By buying WUI, which already had telex contracts, we might more easily begin the dialog needed to open these foreign markets to voice competition.

Along with the deal came an option for a building WUI was leasing in lower Manhattan. I was able to sell that option for $14 million, which was a deal sweetener.

There was a piece of WUI that we didn't want, though, a tele-phone answering service with about 1,500 employees. It didn't fit within our plans so we needed to jettison it. Wayne English, our

CFO said, "I've got just the guy for you - Marty Silver." Marty was a dealmaker and his company, North American Leasing, had taken over some debt and MCI warrants when Bill needed money and the banks had said 'no.' Marty's expertise was in buying anything and everything that was a capital improvement at MCI and leasing it back to us in order to get some short-term financing at very high rates. This got cash into our company quickly. Marty would have leased us back the paint on the walls if he could. (For all I know, he did.)

North American Leasing paid us $7 million for the telephone answering business. Jerry took over Airsignal and built out the cellular business which we sold years later for $120 million. (At one point, when Orville wanted to sell the MCI cellular business, Jerry came to me and suggested that he and I try to raise money to buy it from MCI and give it a go on our own. In hindsight, it was a wrong-headed decision on my part to take a pass, because we could have been at the forefront of the cellular phone business. This was proven when Craig McCaw acquired MCI's position, enhanced it and later sold his company to AT&T for $11 billion.)

MCI got out of the cellular business because we were moving into fiber optics. Orville decided that we needed cash and couldn't build a nationwide optic fiber investment at the same time we were investing in a cellular network. He believed it was just too much for a company of our size to sustain. We were probably a billion dollars in revenue at the time, and Orville was a fairly conservative fellow.

We brought two other people on board in 1982 who were pivotal to MCI's success. The first was Bob Harcharik who had started Tymnet, a packet switching company. Packet networks took customers' data communications, compressed them into little chunks or packets and when a packet was full, sent it out in tight bursts. Because it was sent quickly and in bulk it was a cheap way to send a lot of data. Tymnet leased long distance lines from AT&T and converted them into a packet switching network. Only two other companies were in this business, Telenet and IsoComm, and Bob really understood the technical and business side of the data communications business.

The other person who joined MCI later that year was Vint Cerf, who had spent most of his career as a research engineer. Vint had worked at the Defense Advanced Research Projects Agency, also called DARPA, where he worked with packet switching and figuring out how to link data networks together. Indeed, it was Vint and Bob Kahn who developed the TCP/IP protocols that became the underlying logic on which the entire Internet is now based and for which they both recently received the Presidential Medal of Freedom. Vint would be instrumental in building the company's digital network and the world's first commercial email system which was called *MCI Mail*.

We were rapidly building out the microwave network so we could cover the nation, but were having problems in certain parts of the country. I knew that Bill had experience with satellite communications, and I did too from my days working with COMSAT. I kept harping that at a minimum we ought to have satellite back-up in the event of an outage. I knew that satellites had a time delay which was objectionable to phone users, but it was tested technology. I knew Tom Whitehead at Hughes, and we talked about MCI buying half of a satellite that they were going to launch for cable TV companies which would be using it to broadcast to their local cable outlets. This would allow us to have backup capability for our emerging network. Orville didn't like satellites and neither did Tom Leming, our network senior vice president, who was building out the microwave network. The issue of whether or not to buy satellite capacity caused a huge rift in our top management.

I pushed hard for my point of view. It would cost us about $70 million to invest in two different satellites. It was a good deal because we could use it for data, even though we didn't have a lot of data transmissions at the time. More importantly, we could always lease out the capacity we weren't using to the cable companies because it was pretty clear that they were going to need it. I took the long view despite what others thought.

I convinced Bill, and he worked on everybody else, and finally we agreed that we'd buy half of each of the Galaxy II and III satellites that were being built by Hughes. After we made that commitment, Orville called me aside and warned me, "You've made a big mistake and you've made some enemies here." I was on Orville's bad list now because I had done something that he didn't want to do. I was sure that besides Orville, the only person who didn't like satellites was Tom Leming. My notion of MCI always was that we'd fight it out, but once the leader made the decision then we're all good and we go and we make the best out of it. It didn't work out that way in this case. My decision haunted me until I left the company even though it was, financially at least, an excellent move.

Aside from leasing out any capacity that we didn't need, our treasurer, soon to become CFO, Bill Conway, advised us that we could sell off the tax benefits from the satellites to another company. Just in tax benefits alone, we would be able to recover about half of the investment in the satellites. Jeff Ganek from AT&T, who I brought in to run the satellite business, sold off the tax benefits and also leased excess capacity. I also told him that if the satellites ever didn't fit within our network and business model anymore then he had to sell it off. This would ensure that we weren't wasting resources.

Author (left) and MCI Chairman Bill McGowan watched a 3D movie during a Chairman's Club award meeting in 1988.
Author's collection.

The company had a lot on its plate. Aside from our long distance business over microwave networks, we had the satellites, WUI integration, cellular projects and the biggest issue, of course, was access to the local phone network which the Bell companies still controlled. It was going to cost us a bloody fortune to connect our long distance network to the local phone network so customers could make a call.

I suggested that we hold a strategy session in the spring of 1983, and we did. About 14 people attended. One of the items I brought up concerned access charges, and I made a strong pitch that we should align ourselves with the cable television franchises. As a requirement of their franchise being granted, the newer operators were required by their cities to build an 'institutional network.' This network was available to interconnect all the city departments, but it might also be available for any other use that might be needed in their downtown marketplace. I said to the group: 'The cable franchisees had to build these networks, and they're lying idle most of the time. We could take advantage of them. If nothing else, we could use it as a bargaining chip when we have meetings with the Bell companies about access charges. Even if we don't use these networks, we can have it in our back pocket."

All of our plans required money, so shortly after the strategy session, around June, Wayne came into my office and asked: "Do you believe what you said about all of our opportunities and the costs for getting into cellular, data and international?"

'Yes, I really do,' I said.

He said, "Then let's go talk to Bill about getting more money." We had just received about $400 million in funding, but we needed even more funding if we were to grow.

Bill called Michael Milken at Drexel Burnham and said: "The $400 million was a great deal, but we'll need at least twice that going forward to accomplish what we want to do." At this time, the FCC was planning to hold hearings on access charges, and it didn't look good for us. We would probably be paying much higher rates. We wanted to raise the extra funding before the FCC made a decision that would hurt our bottom line and discourage investors. About three weeks later, in July 1983, I, along with Bill and Dick Sayford, met with Jacques Attali, French President Francoise Mitterrand's right-hand man, about entering the voice business as a partner with the French PTT. It became apparent to us that if we bought about $15 million worth of switches from Compagnie Générale d'Electricité or CGE, it might ease the way for connecting our network to the French telecommunications network for international calls between the U.S. and France. Sitting at Napoleon's desk, Attali delivered the ultimatum: If we ordered the switches, they might consider doing a deal with us. It was that blatant a shakedown. McGowan shook his head and said: "We'll take it under consideration."

We returned to our hotel and Bill got a conference call from Wayne and Michael Milken. "Bill, the funding that you were wondering about," said Mike, "I can get you $2 billion." Bill looked at me and he looked at Dick and repeated what he had just heard. Then he said that we could have the money in a week. Not hesitating, Bill said, "Michael, we'll take a billion, no more." That story became a Harvard Business School case study because it was the first time that any company had raised a billion dollars through junk bonds. It was Milken's coup de grace. The topper of the story was that the FCC had tripled our access fees in twenty days, which caused the stock price to drop from $20 to $6, which would, in turn, have made it nearly impossible to have raised a billion dollars from investors. We were extremely lucky with the timing, and the billion dollars meant that we could expand our business despite our low stock price.

With the increased access charges it became even more important that we begin discussions with cable operators to use their local network. I had known some of them from my time with Subscription TV. We talked with Cox Cable, United Cable and even Ted Turner's cable company in Atlanta. I pitched them: 'We want to connect our voice circuits to your cable network. We could move voice traffic from our customer base to your head-end by using microwave, and then use your head-end to take the traffic to our switching center located downtown. That way, we don't have to do any business with Bell South.' They didn't care for Bell South any more than we did, so they liked the idea.

We ended up in nine different markets with our product called *cablephone* which we demonstrated at the *Western Cable Show* in 1984 in Anaheim. We carried a digital signal from hotels on the Disneyland complex to the top of Anaheim Stadium through cable. We ran the cable to a radio transmitter we put in place of a big spotlight used for night games. From there we pointed it to the window of our Santa Ana switching center to complete access to the MCI network. This dramatic demonstration showed that we didn't need the local phone company to carry digital signals locally.

As we were moving to implement this, we needed to understand more about fiber technology, because we decided that it could one day become the future of our digital network. Fiber cables were able to carry many more transmissions than microwave and were protected from weather because much of it was underground. Fiber could also carry data at higher speeds allowing video and other transmissions that required large bandwidth. In addition, when you buried cables, you could also bury additional cables for relatively little extra cost. This cable could stay unused or 'dark' until you needed it or leased to other carriers.

To help us learn what was available in fiber technology, Tom Leming, the strongest voice advocating fiber as the future of our network, invited me on a tour of European companies who were on the forefront of the technology. We went to CGE and Thomson CSF in France, Siemens in Germany, Ericsson in Sweden then to Plessey in the U.K. where we also visited the British Telecom labs at Martlesham. We soon learned that BT labs was ahead of everybody else in these technologies, but they could never bring it into production. The French always talked about what great technology they had, but they really didn't. Ericsson had some strong technology, but they were all caught up in the fact that they had to export all over the world to make money. We came back with the notion that, indeed, it was clear to us at that point that the Japanese were ahead in fiber optic technology and implementation. We didn't meet with the Japanese then, but we visited Fujitsu on a later trip. Still, from what we had heard and read at the time they were on the cutting edge. They also were very interested in doing business with us, and we were keen on them because their technology seemed superior to that developed by Bell Labs, the research arm of AT&T. Bell Labs had a fiber technology termed 'multi-mode' that needed regeneration every 2-½ miles or so and the transmission rate was about 95 megabits per second. Fujitsu's 'single-mode' technology needed amplification once every 20 miles at a speed of 405 megabits per second. This represented about 6,000 voice circuits and was superior to anything AT&T offered. The choice of Fujitsu was an anathema to the FCC and the American public because it didn't include technology from the United States. Nonetheless, we decided to go with the best technology we could find and made a commitment to build a single-mode fiber network between New York and Washington on rights of way that we got from Amtrak and the CSX railroads.

By 1984, we had the barebones of the matrix. We had voice, data, domestic and international. It was even more important to have these pieces in place now because AT&T and the federal government had agreed that the telephone giant would be broken up in July. The long distance business and the local phone business would be separated. This was both a challenge and blessing for us. With the Bell companies separate and independent from AT&T, it might be even more difficult to gain access to their local lines even though the government mandated that they must give us access at a reasonable rate. Despite the government's order, the local phone companies could give us a hard time with wiring delays and other tactics. Even though they were separate from AT&T, many of the local Bells despised McGowan and MCI because they blamed us for breaking up the Bell System. On a personal level, some of the senior people saw their chances of moving to corporate now ruined because of the breakup, so some of them went out of their way to make life difficult for us. Not all of them, but some of them. The upside for us was that some Bells might realize that they no longer owed allegiance to AT&T, and that we would become a large and valued customer in addition to AT&T. In essence, we could bring them more business than AT&T alone.

Because local access was the chokepoint for our business, we decided to break up MCI into divisions to conform to those of the Regional Bell Operating Companies. This would allow each division to focus on their particular local Bell company and make sure that they were playing by the rules for equal access, that is, giving MCI the same access to the local phone system as AT&T's long distance service. It would allow us to get closer to our customers, too.

It was also a way to shake up some of the malaise that was overshadowing MCI at the time.

My new job was to head up the Mid-Atlantic division, which was located just across the Potomac River in Arlington, Virginia. This was good for my family because we didn't have to relocate. It also would allow me to stay in touch with what was going on at headquarters in Washington, DC.

While I stood by Bill's decision to decentralize the organization, a bold move for any company, I was a bit dismayed by his choice of Bert Roberts as president of the telecommunications subsidiary. Bert was an introvert, led operations and I didn't think he was up to the job. It wasn't as if we were at loggerheads all the time, but we certainly weren't the best of colleagues. He had been at MCI much longer than I had been there and had earned his stripes by building the switching network for the company. Apparently, Orville believed this position was Bert's reward for his service.

Despite his choice of Bert, I still had great respect for Bill. I learned a lot from his management style especially about making decisions. The key thing that I learned during these years was that you had to be buttoned up, but you also had to be willing to just step out and get the job done. And you didn't wait. If you did - if you wanted to syndicate a decision - that was fine, but you made sure that you got it done quickly. We were moving so fast that it was

'Ready, Fire.' There was no time for 'Aim.' You just got right in and pulled the trigger. You used your best judgment and got on with it.

The related thing I learned was how to deal with people's normal tendency *not* to make decisions and move forward but procrastinate and study things to death. Bill spent most of his waking days trying to fight bureaucracy, and I picked that up. Another McGowan lesson was to be counter intuitive. Today, it is sometimes referred to as thinking outside the box but in Bill's case it was a mindset. He claimed that he was successful as a consultant, because he would come into a company and have them do the opposite of what they were currently doing. If salespeople were on commission, he would suggest putting them on salary. If they were on salary, he would recommend they go on commission. About 60 percent of the time, Bill claimed, just shaking things up moved a company forward. If they weren't successful doing what they were doing, what could be wrong with doing just the opposite?

Shaking up MCI the company was part of the reason Bill wanted to decentralize it. I didn't agree with every facet of the plan, but once he made the decision to break us up into seven divisions, that was the way it would be.

One of my red thread strands always is loyalty, and I was on board.

———

Chapter 9

Changing The Face Of The Telecommunications Industry

We established the Mid-Atlantic division in a building in Pentagon City that MCI had bought earlier that year to house the company's back room administrative and financial activities. The next thing I had to do was assemble my team.

The first person I drafted was Larry Bouman, an operations person running all of the switches in the Mid-Atlantic area, even reaching into the Carolinas. He became my vice president of operations.

The next person on my list was Tom Wynne, who was a vice president of sales for the East Coast for MCI. To me, Tom was an obvious choice, but neither Bill nor Orville agreed. Tom had developed a style that many thought too smooth, controlled but not intense enough for the MCI culture.

'Tom,' I said, 'I want you to be the head of sales for my division. But if you do, you're going to be a director, not a vice president.'

Tom's first reaction was, "Why should I do that?" and he was right to say it because it was a step down for him. 'It's either that or you don't have a job,' I responded. This was a very tough meeting for both of us. Sitting in our new office in New Jersey, I laid it out: 'As far as I'm concerned, if you're as good as you think you are, and if you can produce results, pull this thing together in six months, I'll make you a vice president. I'm not going to make you a vice president until you show me results.' He hated that, but accepted the job.

After six months, he took charge and proved his detractors wrong. I made him a vice president.

For my vice president of finance, I interviewed Joe Lawrence who was recommended to me for a job at MCI just before we divisionalized. After 15 minutes I offered him a job. Why? He was a tough Long Island kid with a chip on his shoulder. He was the kind of guy that wasn't going to tell you what you wanted to hear; he was going to tell you what he thought. I wanted that kind of person on my team. Because we were divisionalized, it wasn't a traditional financial position but control and management of costs and reporting - more of a comptroller-type job.

As my general counsel, I hired Bill Marmon, who had been a writer for *Time-Life* and was the bureau chief for *Newsweek* in Cambodia. He then went on to Beirut to cover that area when it became hot. He had a Harvard Law degree and was smart as hell. Some suspected that he may have been a CIA operative and not a journalist as he professed, but it didn't matter.

A theme ran through my hiring. I wanted people with a high level of independence. They also needed the basic knowledge about what made MCI go. They had to understand the DNA of the company. They also had to be quick learners because we were starting almost from scratch. Bouman and Wynne knew the markets they were in; they could be given responsibility and be held accountable. By the same token, the general counsel and CFO were people who were more administrative, but they had to be quick studies and know what was going on in the rest of the company.

Personality-wise, I wanted people who were both flexible and aggressive in getting the job done. I sought those who didn't need someone telling them how to move, self-starters, which was difficult to find in the telecom industry at the time. The vast majority of people in telecom worked for AT&T and companies that modeled themselves in the same way. They made decisions through committees, not on their own. My experience was that when I hired people from AT&T they were always uneasy about working at MCI because the atmosphere was so different from what they knew. Some of them could adapt and walked around with a perpetual smile because they could use their initiative and weren't held back in making decisions. They worked out well. Others from AT&T said they wanted to have the freedom to make decisions but then discovered that they couldn't do it. They would hire three people to do their job instead of saying: "I'm supposed to be doing this job." You could quickly tell who these people were because they would hire a big staff, each with an assistant, and then try to build a structure to support it.

Like Bill McGowan, I wanted people who could make decisions without me and move quickly. I would always say: 'Get it done. And if you can't, if you reach an impasse and you need something to be done, let me know and I'll be there for you, and I'll help you get it done. And, in fact, I'll make the decision. You may not like what I will do, but I'm willing to do that.' It was a Bill McGowan trick to get people to move forward on their own instead of always involving me in their decisions.

My philosophy on mistakes was like Bill's, as well. You could make a mistake but don't make the same mistake twice. You learn by doing, and if you're not making mistakes, you're not trying. This is the same attitude that many companies have today, but at the time it was not common practice. Mistakes were punished at many firms. Also, when people came to me I would always suggest that they think through the opposite side of the problem. It wasn't just because Bill did that, it was my style as well.

Unlike Bill, though, I tried very hard to communicate with people under all circumstances. Bill didn't do so well in some situations, which sometimes seemed enigmatic. He loathed cocktail parties because he despised small talk - unless it was related to MCI or the industry. On the other hand, he could charm people in large groups or even one-on-one with his charisma and affability.

Mid-Atlantic was not the largest division from the standpoint of revenues or profits or anything else for that matter. Partly it was because Mid-Atlantic was in the most intensely competitive telecommunications marketplace at the time. For instance, we took in little Charleston, West Virginia, where MCI made its first big push as did every other new telephone company in the just-established competitive long distance business. We had to be there in the beginning - the FCC had mandated Charleston to host the opening of telephone competition - but did we really want to spend any more resources on such a tiny market just to show the flag?

Our main challenge was keeping the sales force motivated. It was crucial to have the right number of people and set up strong incentive programs, because it wasn't a question of sophisticated engineering sales. They were selling long distance service, which was a relatively simple concept once consumers understood that they had choices other than AT&T. What was difficult, though, was breaking into large corporations. Just before the decentralization, we had landed Merrill Lynch, and it was MCI's largest single customer. More important, that sale gave us the street credibility to go after other large customers, which we did.

Another challenge was not just getting more of a customer's telecommunications budget but being able to support that billing. I would meet with Bell Atlantic and talk about them double-billing us all the time. One time I had set up a meeting with the president of C&P, and I'd bring Joe along with his big box of bills. They would bring along their finance person, and we would square off.

They said: "You haven't paid your bills; we'd like you to pay your bills." Joe would pick up the box and drop it on the table and say, "Here's the bill that you sent us. If you look carefully, you'll see that you billed us three times for the same circuits. Your billing's not worth anything." They would rant and say that double billing wasn't possible because it was a payment system developed by Bell

Labs, but we would show them the bills in black and white and they didn't know how to respond. We had to stand up to them but at the same time let them know that we were both in this together. We were their customers, and if we were successful, they would be successful, but some of them still believed that we were the enemy because of our previous adversarial relationship with AT&T. One exception was Ray Smith, president of Bell Pennsylvania, who invited us to meet so his staff could meet our staff. He understood the reality of our relationship. Ray soon became the CEO of Bell Atlantic and eventually CEO of Verizon. To this day, Ray is a valued and respected friend.

Because of the decentralized nature of the new MCI, presidents could institute their own ideas, but I borrowed a few from Bill. One was anti-nepotism. I hadn't started out with that thought, but I realized that Bill was right. He insisted that no two people in the same organization be married or even related. Having family members in the same place introduces a completely different factor into decision-making, on performance, working with other people, and so forth. As Bill would say, "How would you like it if one of my 16 nephews and nieces was sitting right next to you, having a similar responsibility or being a part of your team? You're always fearful that they're talking to Uncle Bill. You're always fearful that they're getting instructions from Uncle Bill, and you're always fearful that if you step out of line, they're going to tell him." He was right.

Bill forbade office parties. No Christmas parties, and no divisional parties with husbands, wives, girlfriends and boyfriends drinking and carrying on. In the early days of MCI, some guy went off with a female co-worker at a party and got into trouble. Bill said at the time, "We don't need this. We don't need that kind of a diversion from our business focus." He also said: "I happen to be Catholic, so why should I think that all the Jewish people should celebrate Christmas with me?" He had a point.

Author (left) and MCI Chairman Bill McGowan met actress Dinah Shore during a cocktail
party at KCET-TV studios in Los Angeles to celebrate the opening of the 8-part series
Television on PBS, which was sponsored by MCI; 1988.
Author's collection.

I worked very hard, nose to the grindstone. I took the office
space we had, made sure that I wasn't overspending, and I made
certain that everybody was focused on what they should be doing.
I was always around, even on Saturday mornings like we did in
the earlier MCI days. During my tenure as Mid-Atlantic president
our work paid off: we eventually became 30 percent of the overall
company's sales and 50 percent of its profits.

There were several reasons for our success. First, our cost structure was better than the other divisions because we had a more
compact and intense area. Second, the pricing structure was competitive. Third, we nailed down many large accounts and started
the revenue stream going. And fourth, we were right next to the
billing headquarters, so we could make sure that they were doing
their job. We took these advantages, and we generated significant
success out of the division. I also beefed up our federal sales. I
actually brought in a fellow from AT&T named Jerry Edgerton
who did a terrific job selling to the government.

Amid all of this work as division head, I was also involved in the
biggest deal MCI had done to that time.

Satellite Business Services, or SBS, was owned by IBM. As the name suggested, it was a satellite-based system that carried data, a business that we wanted to enter. I said to Bill: 'I know that you like the satellite business, and I think it's the best technology out there for data communications. It doesn't have a lot of gas to it, but this is the only game in town, and we can quickly become a player in the data communications business if you were to buy this from IBM.'

It was a classic IBM situation. They loaded the top management with people who were not pulling their own weight. They were technology people, not business people, so all they did was show how they could lose $10 million a month. It didn't matter whether their revenue was $100 million or, as it was right then, $300 million. They were still going to lose $10 million a month.

Bill's idea was to buy it with equity, so IBM would end up owning a chunk of MCI. He wanted the cachet of having a well-respected name connected with us. That's why Jerry Taylor had done a deal with American Express in 1981, when we were selling the *Express Phone* for American Express members. People could use their American Express card numbers to call through our network. Bill made an overture to John Akers at IBM, laid out how much they were losing and that we would take this loser off their hands. Nothing came of the meeting. Nine months later, though, Akers called Bill and said he would like to talk about it.

The end result was that they sold us SBS for about $360 million in MCI stock. This gave IBM 17 percent of the equity in our company. In addition to that, they agreed to produce $200 million worth of debt for us whenever we needed it.

I headed the integration teams who were trying to figure out how to meld SBS into our company. We really didn't want to be in the satellite business, per se, but take the data transmissions and move them to our terrestrial network, including the fiber network that we were building. There were IBM-class customers sending data over the satellites, and we wanted that business to fill our network. SBS was running at a loss for IBM and its partners, and we figured that we could lower their transmission costs. That would be a plus for them.

A big benefit for us was that it legitimized MCI to be partners with an established and well-respected company like IBM. Bill didn't care what we did with the satellites; his only interest was that IBM had taken a stake in MCI. In fact, the way in which we structured the announcement told that story. The headline read: "IBM buys 17 percent of MCI."

The deal had some drawbacks for us. For one thing, we would have to accommodate the staid IBM culture into our corporate culture. We were opposites. We also took on IBMer Dick Liebhaber to replace Tom Leming who retired. He had fashioned himself as being a technology guru, but he wasn't truly an operating guy. The satellite deal also fomented a rift between Bill and Orville because Orville was somewhat against the transaction. Not only did he dislike satellites, but he thought that IBM's culture would infiltrate ours and slow us down. Orville was conservative, but he understood that MCI had a unique forward-thinking culture that he didn't want to ruin.

I was meeting with Ed Lucente, head of sales for IBM, when I got a call that Bill had a heart transplant. He had been on the waiting list after having sustained a heart attack in 1986. There was no way to prove it, but Bill may have suffered his heart attack and subsequent heart problems from all the business pressure and personal tensions at the company. This was exacerbated by the telecom downturn in late '86 and early '87 which forced MCI to cut 2,000 jobs.

Wall Street was anticipating a lot from us and that was also a reason we were forced to announce a major staff reduction. It was the first time that the company had to cut the workforce. It wasn't just us. The whole telecommunications market was in the bag. There was a lot of competition with all the startup telecom companies, so the margins weren't there as before, and telecommunications was starting to look like a commodity where pricing was the only criteria for a sale. There were continued pressures to invest in infrastructure, and yet the money wasn't coming through that would allow companies to invest. In addition, we still carried a lot of junk bonds on our balance sheet.

Despite the uncertainty and apprehensiveness, our division was doing pretty well. We went from around $200 million to over a billion dollars in sales in about two-and-a-half years. In general, though, the divisional structure was not producing the kind of growth that was expected.

With the rapid growth and then the turndown in the market, coupled with the level of independence they were given, it became very difficult to manage the divisional presidents, which was another reason the new structure wasn't achieving the success we had hoped for. By this time, Orville was out of the day-to-day picture since he had retired, but the board was pressing him back into service to take over Bill's CEO position until Bill could recover. I had been asked to become executive vice president at headquarters as the company was in some chaos.

Before taking the executive VP position I had a conversation with one of the board members, Dick Sayford, who said: "You really have to do this, because it's clear to the board that Bert is having some difficulty in making this happen."

I responded: 'I want you to know that because of Bill's problems and what we're going through, I'll do anything for the company, and I'll be happy to do so. But the net result of what I will do – and I'll bet you a thousand dollars – is that if I end up very successfully helping to turn the company around, Bert will get the sole credit for it.' I reiterated my story about Gelman and how I had made a mistake taking over a position while the real power of the company stayed in limbo only to reappear.

Dick swore that it would not happen, but I said: 'I've heard that before, and I don't want to hear it again. I'll do it, but mark my words, at the end of two years Bert's going think he was a hero.' I was loyal to the company, so I tucked in and took the job despite my misgivings.

Mary Ann was okay with me taking the position but also had reservations about where it might lead. She really liked me being a divisional president, though, because after the Gelman fiasco I was leading real people doing real jobs. She became kind of a mother hen to everybody in the office and did a fabulous job watching out for them. She had a special way of caring for people.

I made some decisions once I got to headquarters. I asked Jerry Taylor to leave his division in Denver and take over the reins at Mid-Atlantic for me. I thought he was the right guy to handle what I was doing. I sent Tom Wynne, who was my VP of sales, to take Jerry's position because it was a much smaller division and focused on sales. Jerry and Tom Wynne were not good friends, so it was a dicey decision on my part. Charlie Skibo, the divisional president based in Atlanta for the Southeast division who had left some time ago, was replaced by Dan Akerson, the head of operations for international. Dan eventually became executive vice president finance, president, then left MCI to run General Instrument. Still later, he became chairman of General Motors. Other presidents, like Gene Eidenberg, left their positions, too. Bill Conway also got an offer from three other people to start a private equity firm called The Carlyle Group, and he was thinking about leaving, which he eventually did.

Tensions remained high at headquarters, but I was doing my job running the divisions on a daily basis. All the line operations including international reported to me as did the corporate sales and marketing function. We restructured the company so that we had me and my organization, Dick Liebhaber who had taken over the transmission systems and information technology as an EVP, Bill Conway as CFO, and all the other corporate functions reporting to Bert. We also had the business of the company managed by an executive committee, which included Bill Conway, Dick, Bert and me. Orville had moved to Monterey, California, after Bill's illness. He carried the title of Co-CEO, and tried to run the company from his base there. He kept an apartment in Washington and attended meetings, but became more like a consultant to the managing committee.

Over the next two years MCI grew as never before. We increased revenues by some $3 billion, we established MCI as the real, heads-on competitor to AT&T in the major national and international accounts, as well as the general marketplace, and we became a data and voice company to be reckoned with and respected throughout our industry. This all happened because of the leadership and efforts of the eight divisional presidents who reported to me: Nate Kantor in the Northeast, Jerry Taylor – Mid-Atlantic, Dan Akerson – Southeast, Frank Harkins – Southwest, Ted Trimmer – Pacific, Ron Spears – Midwest, Tom Wynne – West, and Seth Blumenfeld – International. I would also mention Jonathan Crane who came to us to head an effort to build our National Accounts Program. This team competitively built MCI into a world leading telecom player and made me and the rest of the management team look truly successful.

Amid all this tumult, after we got the company back on track and all the divisions growing nicely, Bert decided he wanted to manage the divisions directly again. McGowan, recovered from his heart transplant, asked me to go back in the role of handling strategy because the company seemed to be losing direction. We really didn't know where we were going and I viewed this change as somewhat of a demotion. Nonetheless, I began to actively try to find merger partners while developing close ties with BT and wireless carriers in an effort to search out the next major move in the industry for MCI.

Bert decided to pick up the BT relationship as a possible ally going forward, and I started to feel like the odd man out in trying to secure new relationships for the company as well as a good future for myself. Looking for other ways to redefine success, Bert also decided to make a major acquisition to further cement his leadership of MCI. He collaborated with Dan Akerson, who had replaced Bill Conway when he left MCI about a big deal that he might do - the acquisition of Telecom USA. I knew the company well, and had advised against the deal earlier. I had studied the company and had become close to several executives who regaled me with many stories of the disfunctionality in the organization. I had modeled and reviewed the possible combinations in great detail and between the price they were asking, and the problems that integration would present, I was convinced that the company wasn't right for MCI. There was no possible way that we could achieve a return on that investment worthy of doing the deal. Nonetheless, once Bert and Dan secured that decision from the board, in the spring of 1989, I knew my credibility was clearly diminished, and my time at MCI was, unfortunately, coming to an end. At first I thought they knew something about Telecom USA that I didn't, but then I realized that they were wrong. I believed it would be a terrible acquisition, but Bert and Dan were adamant about it. Several years later, I believe my assessment was proven correct.

Bill and I had conversations about the situation, but he was too ill to keep his hand on the company's rudder. Orville made it clear to me that the MCI ship was now Bert's to run.

It was very sad to watch this happen because Bill and I shared the same sense of MCI's future. We were very close in that regard. Bert was quite the opposite. The difference was that Bert was no-nonsense, by the numbers, tough with people. I was more of the customer-focused person who really wanted to get out selling and promoting MCI's future as well as the technology of the company. To accomplish that, we had to engage clients by sponsoring sporting events and golf tournaments, which fostered personal and business relationships. I was always out there doing things which were viewed by Bert and Orville as unnecessary activities. When you looked at it, though, these activities landed us large clients and resulted in MCI becoming a major factor in the corporate world. Bill wasn't a glad-hander, but he understood the importance of getting close and personal with customers. It was the company's greatest growth period, and I like to think that I had a hand in that success.

However, with Bill no longer involved with the company, and Bert taking it over, MCI was becoming a different company. It was not the place it had been, lean and aggressive, forward thinking. It was bureaucratic with political infighting and people jockeying for power instead of putting the company first. It was exciting to know that we had built a great company, made business history, and it was sad as well to see that it had lost direction because of some people's penchant for power and personal ego over long-term shareholder interests. All my concerns expressed earlier when I came back to headquarters from being a divisional president had, unfortunately, come to pass.

Bert and I came to a mutually acceptable agreement that I would leave right after our offsite strategy planning session that year. It was one of the hardest meetings for me to chair, and I announced my departure at the end of the session.

I was loyal to the company and to many of my colleagues, but no longer had respect for those running the company. I was concerned about the direction in which they were heading, and in August, 1990, I left MCI with great sadness. Unfortunately, MCI went into a difficult period, its strategic direction was lost and principles got washed away in ill-advised deals. The company would head later into bankruptcy along with parent WorldCom and with it went its brand and culture. Its legacy would live on, however, with many of those left behind who would go on to pursue other business opportunities.

I was proud that I had been a part of something that had changed the face of an entire industry which resulted in how the nation and the world eventually viewed telecommunications. We were involved in helping to start the wireless industry and the internet at their virtual birth. And, the world was in a telecom revolution allowing competitive players to break the monopolies that had dominated the industry for a hundred years.

———

Chapter 10

Simple, Fair and Inexpensive

Once again, now at age 50, I was looking for my next management role.

My friend Cal Andringa, a former treasurer at Marriott, had rented an office in Georgetown, and we shared space along with some other people including his accountant. I returned to consulting which was somewhat of a letdown because I had ostensibly been running most of MCI for two years. When people heard that I had left the company, I began receiving calls from other telecom companies wanting me to consult with them, helping to sort out their strategies. I got calls from British Telecom, France Telecom, GTE, Cox Communications and other large companies. I was grateful for the work but not happy about my situation.

In the spring of 1991, I received a call from Adam Solomon of Warburg Pincus, one of the original venture capital firms that had become a standout success in the field, who wanted to talk about a small company called LiTel. After the break-up of AT&T, companies sprang up to build smaller versions of MCI, handling regional traffic that the newly-formed local Bell companies were not legally allowed to take on. The local Bells were only permitted to operate within areas known as LATAs, or Local Access and Transport Areas. LiTel was one of the companies taking advantage of this once-in-a-lifetime opportunity to connect the LATAs so calls could be completed. They competed for this regional business against long-distance companies including MCI, AT&T and Sprint.

In fact, there was a group of about eight of these regional companies who had set up a consortium they called the National Telecommunications Network or NTN. They agreed to conduct business among themselves and had established rates for terminating calls in each other's region. This gave them the look of a nationwide long-distance carrier.

LiTel, headquartered in Ohio, was planning to build fiber across Ohio and into Illinois and Michigan. They raised money - all of these companies were able to do so fairly easily - and they built themselves up to about $140 or $150 million in revenues, but they needed more cash. In 1989 they turned to Michael Milken - it was his last high-yield deal before being indicted and going to prison - who brought in private equity firm Warburg Pincus, which was now their largest investor. Two years later, Warburg Pincus became unhappy with LiTel management, especially CEO Larry McLernon, who seemed convinced that he was the second coming of Bill McGowan and believed that he could build another MCI. From what I had heard, he was unbridled by his board and allowed to invest in things that were unrelated to the company's core business, like video technology to be used in banks. He had all these projects that were yielding nothing; they were just sucking up cash. McLernon had also neglected the lucrative residential telephone market.

Adam told me how Warburg Pincus had sunk about $35 million into LiTel and was now worried about their investment. They were uneasy because LiTel had not met budgets, kept spending money and management was not responding to Warburg's instructions.

It all came to a head in May 1991, after a board meeting, when their CFO, Larry Wolfe, was walking to his car with Adam and another board member, Jim Bartlett of Primus Partners. At the meeting they had just attended McLernon's talk was upbeat, the future was rosy and their problems would be short-lived. He bragged how one of their new major investors, ItalCABLE, was supportive of the company.

Now, on the way to their cars, Wolfe said: "Oh, by the way, Larry didn't mention it, but I think I should tell you. We're not going to be able to make our payments on the debt in June because we're out of cash."

This was part of what prompted Adam to ask me: "Is there anything you can do to help me at this stage?" I said, 'Adam, I know that company. They came to me three or four times to get financing at MCI, and there was no way we were going to support them. But, if you really want me to, I'll take a look and tell you what I think. Let me take a look at the numbers; I'll talk to some folks, and I'll get some understanding of the true situation.'

"In the meantime," he said, "I've already hired some other people to help sort it out." Adam was bringing in some turnaround consultants to assess the damage and see what kinds of fixes were possible.

I finally said, 'I will talk with McLernon. I'll do it as an advisor to you. I'll go to Columbus, talk to him and some key people, and then I'll tell you what I think. Ok?'

I spent an entire day in Columbus, and McLernon played the 'we're both Irish' card which didn't endear him to me. I didn't feel he had a strong grasp of where the industry was headed or his company's role in it.

Afterwards, I told Adam straight out: 'You are going to have to keep pouring in money. They are building a bigger and bigger hole with no way to be profitable by doing things the way they're doing them.' Many parts of the company were dysfunctional. Revenues weren't coming in, and they hadn't stopped spending on projects unrelated to their core business. They had a former telephone company person who didn't understand sales but was managing their sales effort. He had the outdated notion, which was common among phone companies like AT&T, that customers should be considered as 'ratepayers' and sales simply meant taking orders.

There was no sense of cohesiveness in the company at all. In fact, the executive suite was on a separate floor set off by security doors from the rest of the headquarters. It was inaccessible to the rest of the employees. Management was living in their own world, and they didn't spend any time with the rest of the company. It was 'would be' entrepreneurs gone wild.

Author (left), Marshall Hanno and Tom Wynne received a gift from the sales staff during the first Chairman's Club event marking LCI's transition to new leadership; 1992.
Author's collection.

Adam wanted me to take over the company, and I said I would consider it, but I had a number of conditions. 'It will take me six months to know if I can save the company. I'm going to live in Washington and will commute for the time being. I'll get an apartment in Columbus, but I'm going to keep my house in Washington, and I'm still going to keep a little company, Universal Telecommunications, Inc., that I put together for investment purposes. I'd like you to put up 90 percent of a fund, and I'll put up 10 percent, and we'll have this side deal where we'll do some investing.' This would allow me some cover in case things didn't work out. They would put in around $100,000, which was seed money for some entrepreneurial ventures.

Based on my previous experiences, the most important condition was that McLernon had to leave before I arrived. I was not going to repeat the debacle at Gelman where I came on the scene and the CEO was still occupying his office and the board wouldn't get rid of him even though they had promised to do so. I also wanted to bring in several of my own people.

Warburg Pincus agreed to all of my conditions.

McLernon left on July 1, and after the July 4th weekend I showed up and made the speech in the cafeteria that garnered me a standing ovation and appreciation from employees. For the first time they had a management that was being straight with them about the company's perilous financial condition.

There were three people I wanted to hire right off the bat. The first was Tom Wynne. By the time I had left MCI, management was firing a lot of people that they didn't like. Not because they were incompetent; they just didn't care for them. Tom really knew how to organize and lead a sales force and would be a great asset for us.

The second was Marshall Hanno, who worked with Tom many years earlier in Chicago where he handled national accounts for MCI. When Ron Spears, the Mid-West president was targeted for a change, Marshall decided to join us and was a strong complement to Tom because he managed the sales force while Tom was the charismatic leader.

The third was Joe Lawrence, who was my CFO when I was president of MCI's Mid-Atlantic region. Joe had become close to Jerry Taylor, who took over the division after I left. When the company was restructured, and Jerry was slated to take on the residential business, Joe decided to stay even though he was apprehensive, and rightfully so, about the changes taking place at MCI.

After I introduced myself and gave my speech, I went to the executive floor and studied the architecture. Not only were there two ominous large wooden doors shutting off the executive suite, but there was a long and torturous walk to the CEO and CFO's offices. There were two sets of doors that closed off top management's offices from everybody else. The first one closed off the executive suite offices. The second door closed off the CEO and the CFO. It was an absurd configuration that smacked of a siege mentality.

I called the people who were responsible for managing the building. 'When I come in tomorrow morning, this wall is going to be gone, these doors are going to be gone. The third floor's executive section is going to be as open as the rest of the company.'

I was making a statement that I was accessible and available. If there was one thing I had to do, it was communicate. I started the process of rebuilding the company beginning with communication. Every month I called everybody together and told them how we were doing.

The other change I made was to get a new name for the company. No longer would it be LiTel, which had prompted some people to call the company 'Lie Tell.' The new name was LCI International. I took some ribbing that it was one letter earlier in the alphabet than MCI - and therefore a better company - but the new moniker had nothing to do with my old company. It was simply the initials of the parent company Lightwave Communications, Inc.

Within three weeks we had to fire 20 percent of the workforce. I had said in my cafeteria speech that we would be letting employees go, perhaps as many as 25 percent. Naturally, people were upset, but they weren't blindsided.

At the end of the sixth week, I met with John Vogelstein, Warburg's CEO – the person who really convinced me to take on LiTel – to offer a briefing on our progress and let them know the status of their investment. It was a bit ahead of when I thought I would be reporting to them, but we felt we had a handle on the situation.

'I'm far enough into it, and I think I know enough about it, that from everything I can see we can save it,' I said.

"How much is it going to cost?" Vogelstein asked.

'Based on what we see right now, we're probably going to need about $35 million in new cash to get the company back on its feet.'

"When will you need it?" Vogelstein asked, which was his tacit commitment to me. My equally tacit commitment to him was: 'I will let you know.'

That was the beginning of a financial, business and interpersonal relationship we formed with Warburg Pincus that eventually would make our company, and the Warburg fund that owned it, a success.

They already had about that much money in the company, so it was not a small investment for that period, the early 1990s. The investment came from a fund of about $900 million; I believed that they had already written down their first investment to zero. They also wouldn't have to put up the entire $35 million because Primus had 10 percent of it, so they could pony up $30 or $33 million of the $35 million I wanted if necessary.

The irony of the situation was that at the same time Vogelstein was trying to save Mellon Bank, which was the senior note holder on this particular investment. This was during the Savings & Loan crisis, so the financial industry was under great pressure. Mellon was trying to unload the company because they figured it was a bad debt. Their investment committee believed there was no evidence that the bank would get its money back, that we simply couldn't come back from the dead. I was trying to convince Vogelstein that we could bring it back, that it could be profitable with the right management and an infusion of money. Mellon was looking at the past reports and kept telling Warburg to remove us from their portfolio. This went back and forth for some time. They put a lot of pressure on us.

We settled on a classic workout where we would at least pay back the interest on the loan in a timely manner. I also got all of the covenants sorted out with some minor exceptions. We had our sales people scrambling to bring in new business quickly because whenever you're in a workout with a bank, no other bank is going to give you money, and we needed cash. After about 20 months, in the midst of some tough negotiations with our lenders, we were forced to borrow from TransAmerica, which was a 'vulture lender' and an asset manager. It cost us the equivalent of about 42 percent for their money although, as it turned out, we only needed it for three months.

In a TV commercial for LCI the author acted as the company spokesperson,
which was a new idea at the time; 1996.
Author's collection.

I felt that we could turn this ship around through simple hard work and strict cost controls. Aside from letting people go, I found a lot of wasteful spending. Not only had I jettisoned McLernon's ill-conceived technology programs, like the video business, but I found a lot of other holes to seal like his apartment in New York City.

I knew that the network was pretty solid, and that the workers who were left could run switches. It was not rocket science, but it took a commitment from management and a back-to-basics attitude on everyone's part.

I rented an apartment in downtown Columbus, and Mary Ann would visit for a week or weekend and then return to Alexandria. About a year into it, we rented a house and furnished it so it would be a home away from home for us.

Within two years, we had taken the company from the brink of default in 1991 to going public in May 1993. Out of the funds from the IPO, I paid off TransAmerica. By now, the market was responding very well to us and we were able to make some acquisitions to extend our network. By '94, we had fiber routes east to New York and south to Washington. We went to Kansas City and out to Chicago. We started to lease lines in the rest of the country from other carriers. By '95, '96, we were a nationwide carrier, and we actually began to sell service internationally, too. We entered new technologies, and were one of the first companies to put frame relay technology into the backbone for our corporate clients. This was important technology because it was an extremely efficient way of using Internet protocol technology to move large amounts of data across networks. We were starting to do some other creative things beyond simply selling telephone minutes. For example, we created service packages that offered volume parameters and guarantees of performance.

Singlehandedly, we changed the entire industry's pricing structure.

Our residential phone business was growing nicely. We were ready to start charging 14-cent minute flat rate increments which nobody else was offering at the time. We called our program *One-Four America.*

Our other huge selling point would rely on new technology in our switches that allowed software to do something that none of the big telephone companies could do – charge in increments of less than a minute. All of the big companies rounded up to the next minute. It was a big selling point for us to say "we're going to charge you in six-second increments." We expected to make a lot of money with this feature because no one else had it.

First, however, we needed an advertising campaign. I got together with a local advertising firm named for their leader, Ron Foth, and I said to him, 'We want to get some publicity on the company because we really have to expand. We have a new set of programs that we've put together, one of which is to sell a flat-rate minute. Also, we're not going to round up to the nearest minute like everyone else. We're charging in six-second increments.

So we're going to initiate a campaign to try to convince people that they're getting ripped off by the other phone companies.'

I had no trouble convincing him that this was new and unique and never done before in the history of telephone service. He offered some special ideas of his own. "Brian," he said, "if you don't mind, I'd like to come in and bring my camera guys with me. I would like you to sit at your desk, and I'll just ask you questions. We'll talk through this whole campaign. We may talk for several hours and we'll come up with the major points that you think are important for us to include. I'll go back to the studio, look at the footage and see what we can do."

I did as he suggested, and two weeks later he returned to see me. "I want to show you something," Ron said. He had a one-minute advertisement that he had pieced together from our conversation. It was me, sitting at my desk, looking into the camera and explaining how we could save customers money. It was the beginning of a series of similar advertisements that were extremely effective. The commercials grew more sophisticated and professional, but it was still me talking to potential customers. I joked at the time that I became the spokesperson because I was the cheapest talent we could get, but having the CEO of a company speaking to potential customers was a new idea at the time. As we looked at the footage and considered the value proposition, we concluded that beyond the *One-Four-America* branding, that the terms *Simple, Fair and Inexpensive*, were totally compelling and should be branded with the LCI name. *SFI* became a byword and a brand for our residential service.

We still couldn't afford network advertising time, so we continued with local ads in different markets. We were just starting to buy time on CNN for about $3 million a year, which was lot for us, but it still didn't give us the best bang for the buck if we were to go national.

However, we got more than our money's worth because of an unexpected news event. One of the first days that we ran our commercials was the same day that O.J. Simpson was riding down the freeway in his white SUV with the police trailing behind him. CNN had constant coverage of the chase when they flashed to a commercial of me talking about saving money on phone service. It was a serendipitous event, and we got a lot of calls on our toll-free lines.

Tom Wynne had an idea how we could get even more exposure. "I've got this crazy idea," he said. "We're going to sponsor an Indy car."

'No, we're not,' I responded. 'There's no way that I'm going to sponsor guys with cigarettes rolled up in their T-shirts. It's not our market.' I couldn't help but recall when Ron Spears ran MCI's Mid-West division and saw $2 million go down the drain when their Indy car hit the wall.

But Tom had a deal.

"Jack Nicklaus, whose company is Golden Bear, did a swap with somebody and they got a million dollars worth of time on CNN. They have offered us a deal where if we put a million dollars into a race car team to cover the first six months of the season and be the primary sponsor, they would give us the million in airtime and our name will be up on the side of the car. At the end of six months, we can decide if we want to continue our sponsorship, and if we do, it will cost another million dollars for the team."

I couldn't turn it down. It would be excellent exposure for less than we were paying for air time.

Our first race was a road race in Miami. I didn't know a lot about racing, so I asked Tom to travel there and watch the race and keep an eye on our team. Shortly after the race started, he phoned me. "Our guy hit the wall at the end of the second lap, so he's not in the race anymore." I said, 'Oh, good choice, Tom.'

The next race was in Phoenix and again I asked Tom to attend the race. He said that because of our deal with Nicklaus, we were also a co-sponsor of the race. That meant we had signboards that would be seen on television. 'I hope you have a better race than the last one,' I told him. I was watching the race on television and around the seventh lap our Brazilian driver, Andre Ribeiro, ran into the wall. But the good news was that he hit the wall right under the LCI signboard. He was not hurt, and we got a lot of screen time, but we were out of the race again.

The next race was in Long Beach. We had scheduled a recognition event for our sales people on Friday and Saturday in Phoenix, and the race in Long Beach was on Sunday. Tom convinced Mary Ann and me that we had to see firsthand the race in Long Beach. In order to get there we had to get up at 4 a.m., get on a plane in Phoenix, go to Tucson and then go to L.A. Somebody was going to meet us in L.A. and take us to the track. If that schedule wasn't bad enough, once we arrived in L.A. the person picking us up crammed the two of us and our luggage into a Honda Civic. He got us to the race course and we wanted to check into the hotel but couldn't drive to the doorway because the hotel was located inside the racetrack. We had to stop about a half mile away and use carts to lug in our luggage. At this point, Mary Ann wasn't even speaking to me.

I decided to invite to the race a friend of mine named Joe Wallach who was from Brooklyn and now lived part-time in Beverly Hills and the rest in Sao Paulo. Joe had built Global TV for the wealthy Marino family in Brazil and was now a partner of mine in a small venture capital company we had established in Brazil.

It would not only be fun to spend time with Joe and his wife, but he could act as an interpreter between our driver Andre and us because Joe spoke perfect Portuguese. Mary Ann was still upset with me for dragging her to a car race, but while I was checking in she wandered off, apparently curious about a high-pitched whine that caught her attention. It was the sound of cars warming up on the track. I found her a few minutes later with her nose against the glass watching the cars, and she seemed to be quite intrigued by the goings-on. Still, she was annoyed with the whole situation, and it didn't get better. We had just stowed our luggage in our room, hung up our clothes and were on our way down in the elevator when racecar legend A.J. Foyt got on. He was overbearing, obnoxious, making all kinds of off-color comments, and Mary Ann gave me a look and said: "So, this is the kind of people you're into now?"

We headed to the pit area to watch some more warm-ups along with Joe and his wife Doreen when our car pulled in. It was a beautiful car with the latest Honda technology.

Andre got out of the driver's seat and was talking to Joe. Andre came over to introduce himself, and he was out of Brazilian central casting, handsome, with dark curly hair. Joe said to me that Andre spoke perfect English, so no translator was necessary, and that Andre's brother Lincoln Pereira worked for our venture capital company in Brazil.

Andre introduced himself to Mary Ann in a charming and suave way, and she was hooked. He put her in the seat of the racecar, explained everything to her and got her involved. I could just see her turning to butter. Her demeanor softened, and she was no longer put off by the racing scene.

The man who owned the racing team was from New Zealand. I really liked Steve Horne and what he had to say about the sport and the marketing possibilities for LCI. My thoughts went from 'what are we doing here?' to understanding an entire marketing campaign including sponsoring a second car if our sales force was able to use the cars to bring in additional business.

It turned out to be a profitable decision for us. We had four separate programs that exploited the racecars. First, our residential program had sales people at booths taking orders for services, giving out T-shirts, posters and using the cars as a way to get customers excited and in the door. The second program was for our small business customers and was aimed at every smaller company at the racetrack. These included all of the suppliers providing refreshments, track services and other products and services. We had a team of people dedicated to this segment of racetrack activity sales. The third program was our national accounts team who were focused on getting business out of large companies at the track like Firestone and Honda. We also had a fourth program which was a hospitality program. This was set up so that as races moved from city to city, our large accounts in those locations could bring *their* customers to the race track. To keep it from becoming just a giveaway ticket program, we were adamant that the direct account representative had to be there and the customer had to be his company's lead executive.

Mary Ann and I were stationed at the hospitality suites all weekend. It was not only important for large account customers to see us and talk with us, but it was important for the sales team to see us there. Eventually, Mary Ann enjoyed herself, and I got into it, too. I learned about racing, which was something I would never have been exposed to if not for our racing programs.

Driver Andre Ribeiro (left), Mary Ann Thompson (seated) and author prior to the LCI car's first race in Long Beach in 1995.
Author's collection.

Every Monday morning after a weekend race, we reviewed what was accomplished. As unbelievable as it sounds, I could attribute $25 million in new business the first year and $38 million the second year to the racing program, and it only cost us about $5 million.

We ended up sponsoring two cars and got into the Indy *Lite Series* and the Indy race itself. That year for the *Indianapolis 500* we had two cars with LCI's logo on their sides. I watched the race with Tom. One car was driven by Scott Goodyear. Andre drove the other.

After a long, intense and successful effort, with only 14 laps left, both cars were one and two. Then, Andre's car ingested a wrapper from a hot dog and it overheated the engine and it cut out on him. He was out of the race. Now, with five laps left, Scott Goodyear, leading the race, slowed when he spotted a yellow flag. Like his fellow drivers, he held his position in preparation for the restart. He remained in the number one position. As the race restarted, everyone expected the pace car to pull aside at over 100 miles per hour, so as not to slow down the racers, and they would restart the race. This time, however, the pace car didn't accelerate but actually slowed and Scott, seeing the green flag and lights, roared by it as it pulled slowly off to the side. Track officials ruled that he jumped the gun and committed a foul. He countered that he had seen the green lights and wasn't about to slow down and lose his number one position. They black flagged him, withdrew his position and stopped scoring him. He ended up losing the race even though he was ahead of everybody. To this day, I believe it was because he was a Canadian driving a Honda. The Indy establishment liked Hoyt and Andretti. They liked all of the people who had won, but to have a Canadian win was a no-no. Worse than that, it was the first year that there was a Honda engine - a Japanese car - in the race.

I had to console him for a long time. I felt so bad for Scott. He really had won the *Indianapolis 500*, and it was taken from him. Only a few years earlier, he was nosed out in the closest race in Indy history. Unfortunately, two losses like this form a huge negative in the racing business, and time really doesn't heal the pain for drivers.

Andre went on to win several important races: *New Hampshire*, the first *Indy/Brazilian Grand Prix*, and the *Michigan 500*. These were all large, highly respected races, and he won them all.

For our business purposes, winning or losing didn't matter that much. Our logoed race cars brought in a lot of new customers and kept current customers engaged. The program really spoke to the issue of trusting your people to bring new ideas to you and to be open. Many executives dismiss new ideas because they don't fully understand them. I knew nothing at first about racing, even had a bias against it, but realized that it could work for us.

With our success in bringing new business in with our race cars, Bert Roberts from MCI decided to follow our lead. He poured about $29 million into sponsoring an Indy team, but without intense, real executive presence and involvement, it seemed to be just money down the drain. Many executives are enamored by the glitz of racing, football or soccer and sponsor teams and events so they can get close to the racers and players. They want to hobnob with celebrities but they're very often wasting the company's money and resources. So many companies have bad deals that don't pay for themselves. I knew that whether we won or lost races, the promotion would not only pay for itself but bring in large amounts of revenue. If there's anything that I'm passionate about, it's getting a return for what you put in. That's the only way you can build a stable and profitable company. You've got to watch every shareholder dollar you spend. You have to listen to what your people have to say and create opportunities for them to do things for the company and themselves that they didn't know they could do.

Another personal benefit of having Indy cars was meeting Roger Penske. He and I were the only CEOs of good-sized companies at the track every week and deeply involved in the program. He owned his Penske truck rental and Detroit Diesel at the time and was turning it around as I was turning around LCI. We joked about my ads and discussed the business issues surrounding Indy car racing. To this day, we remain close friends.

Another important program at LCI - and I didn't know anyone else doing it - concerned bonuses. I insisted that we pay bonuses quarterly instead of annually like other companies. I thought of bonuses differently, not only as a way to reward good performance quickly - although it certainly served that purpose - but as a management feedback mechanism. It forced managers to assess how their people were doing on a regular basis. Not just assess them, but pick out the winners and the losers and reward the winners and try to help the losers to become winners. You don't do that by just ignoring people for a year and then at the end of the year telling them, 'You messed up back in July and now you're done.' You just don't do that to people. It's not fair. I believe that you have to force managers to manage, because the hardest thing to do is look somebody in the eye and tell them that they're doing a bad job. Managers, or most anyone for that matter, don't want to hurt someone's feelings, yet it's the best thing you can do.

People often ask me: "How are you able to fire somebody?" I always answer: 'Because it's not necessarily a bad thing to do. If people are not performing and you sit back and don't say anything to them you're doing them and the investors a disservice. I consider it a success when people that I have let go come back to me later and say that it was one of the best things that happened to them. And that has happened to me quite often over the years.

I never wanted to do the long evaluations that HR people often prefer. It's too complicated and unnecessary. I like a simple four-layer system to evaluate performance: star on top, then one, two, three. You mostly see 10 percent in the star category, 20 percent in the one, 50 percent in the twos and the rest are at the bottom. I told my managers how much money was in our bonus pool; the total money was based on how well the company was doing. I allocated the money to managers, and they rewarded their people based on the four-layer system. I said that I didn't care how they did it - they could use a computer program if they wanted - but they had to confront people who were only a three and explain how they could move up to a one or two. Or, they had to tell them that they were going to be let go if they didn't improve.

Every quarter I would take 15 minutes and tell all employees the size of the bonus pool based on the company's performance.

The better they performed, the larger the bonus pool and the better they did individually, the higher their bonus.

The whole program didn't take a lot of time, and it helped move people upward, to perform better, to feel better about their performance and their place in the company.

Quarterly bonuses make so much sense. When other companies conduct an annual performance review, sometimes they forgot how badly an employee had done back in June or May. The other thing that happens is that people wait until the last quarter to work their tail off for the bonus when they should have been improving all year. You also sometimes hear people say, 'I'll wait until I get my bonus, and then I'm gone.'

Often in business, the simplest ideas are best, but people don't always use them.

There's no question in my mind that rewarding good performance and coaching poor performance was one of the main forces that drove LCI to prosperity.

I also insisted that everyone at the company, not just executives, had stock options. People would tell me that employees don't understand options, but that's not true. They understood that if the company did well, they were not only rewarded by being part of a successful team, but that they were monetarily rewarded, too.

Options were the vehicle by which we told people that they were share owners too, that they weren't just employees. And as long as people looked at their jobs as simply being an employee of the company, you were going to lose. They had to be part of it, not just an employee, but an owner. Of course everyone's different, and some are not going to respond to that, but if you get up in front of people and say, 'We're coming on to hard times right now; we've got to slow down over here; we're trying to get this thing going over here; we've got to make sure everybody tightens their belt. And if you don't tighten the belt that means someone's going to have to go. If you don't want to see the guy next to you go, and if he doesn't want to see you go, then you've got to get together and figure out how to make things better because you're an owner; I'm an owner and you're an owner. We're all owners, and we're in this together.'

George Kappaz, President & CEO, COMSAT (left); Helio Castroneves, IndyCar Champion; Roger Penske, Chairman, Penske Corporation and Tim Harmon, CFO and major investor, COMSAT at an Indy 500 Race; May 2010.
Author's collection.

Why don't more companies do this? Because they build up structures where every decision is discussed to death and nobody really takes responsibility for anything. If you get 15 people to make sure that what you're doing is the correct way to do it - based on some bureaucratic rule book - it means that nobody can be responsible for failure, and nobody can take credit for success. You stifle creativity and entrepreneurship. I remember consulting with a CEO who said she wanted all of her executive team to make salaries within $2,000 of each other. I said, 'You've got to have somebody who's making more and somebody who's making less. Otherwise you're not realistically assessing the importance of a position or a person.'

By 1996, LCI was a thriving success approaching $1 billion in revenues. By that time, I had also taken on the additional role as Chairman of COMPTEL, the association of competitive tele-com companies, and we were finally getting new telecom legisla-tion intended to rewrite the book on how the industry would be treated and regulated going forward. The Telecom Act of 1996 became law. It gave legitimacy to competition for customers' local access lines.

As we were negotiating that act, I brought into LCI Mark Shriver, Eunice and Sargent Shriver's son who was a Maryland state representative (a part-time role). When he wasn't doing that, I wanted him to lay the groundwork in LCI for a competitive local exchange service offering. It was a win/win strategy where Mark could bring to us the sensitivity we needed in this public policy arena while we could help him to understand the essence of doing business in the private sector. It worked.

As Mark moved us toward that business, we also had the great fortune to bring in Anne Bingaman who had helped develop the essence of the Telecom Act as Assistant U.S. Attorney General for Anti-Trust matters. Anne had decided to leave the Justice Depart-ment, and we enticed her to join us to bring strength and cred-ibility to our local competitive efforts as she built a new business for LCI.

From 1996 to 1998, we aggressively and sensibly built our abil-ity to meet our customers' local and long distance business needs for both voice and data communications.

Against this backdrop, by 1998, LCI was becoming a powerhouse in the telecom business with revenues approaching $2 billion and expanding both domestically and internationally. Our equity value and share price clearly reflected that success.

One of my previous partners, Paul Tierney, from our Brazil-ian venture capital firm, was a huge soccer fan, so he, I, and some others invested in the D.C. United soccer team when they needed funds to get started. We did it for fun but also to give back to the community. George Soros was the major investor, and the rest of us took minority positions. I still had lots of equity in MCI stock, so I was still doing well financially - on paper at least.

Phil Anschutz, who had made his fortune in Wyoming oil, not only invested in railroads, real estate and entertainment, but he also became a co-founder with us of Major League Soccer. He owned soccer teams as well as other professional sports teams. He had bought the Los Angeles and Denver soccer franchises. I got to know Anschutz through my partial ownership of D.C. United but had met him previously on several occasions through his involvement in the telecommunications business. One of his early investments, Southern Pacific, had been an early provider of telecommunications services by virtue of installing cables, later microwave towers and still later installing fiber along the railroad's right-of-way to become one of the nation's first national fiber networks. The Southern Pacific Communications Corporation, as its subsidiary was called, was owned by United Telecom in Kansas City and was bought in 1983 by the GTE Corporation. The deal included a satellite company and the Switched Private Network Telecommunications group known as Sprint, the forerunner of the company we know today.

Phil called me and said he would like to get together. We met in New York where he introduced me to Joe Nacchio, who had been an executive at AT&T and had built a reputation as a tough guy from his younger days in Brooklyn. Some considered him a thug in a three-piece suit because of his brash behavior at AT&T where he became president of their business division. During meetings, Nacchio was prone to angry outbursts and often criticized CEO Robert Allen. AT&T eventually fired Nacchio in a nasty departure reportedly denying him millions in benefits that he claimed he was owed. Nacchio had now hooked up with Anschutz, who had started to rebuild a nationwide fiber network that he was now calling Qwest on the same Southern Pacific rights-of-way.

Qwest was growing rapidly and was a Wall Street darling with a huge market cap but only about $200 million in revenue. At LCI, we were at about $2 billion revenue, but that didn't stop Anschutz from making a run at us. We had an excellent board, including George Perrin, John Vogelstein, Bill Connell, Doug Karp, Jim Bartlett, Dick Cavanagh, and basketball star Julius Erving. I met Julius at a university board where we both served. He wasn't just a celebrity athlete. I found his insights to be unique and his ability to play a role on a board as effective. He was on the board of Coca-Cola in Philadelphia and a couple of banks. During meetings he often would say, "Wait a minute. That's too complicated for most shareholders to understand. Can you make it simpler for me?" That gave him the role of representing the 'little guy,' which I appreciated. That point of view can be a useful factor to help work though some issues before the board.

Nacchio and Anschutz came at LCI, and I tried to fend them off. Others on the board including Julius and Dick didn't want to sell out to Qwest either. We believed that LCI could continue to grow, accomplish great things in the world of telecom and be the model of a modern, well-run corporation. There was some of my ego here, of course. I wanted to see how far I could take LCI, because I believed in the structure that we had built. In many ways, there was no other company like it. In my heart I knew that there was no limit to what it could become.

My duty as CEO, however, compelled me to bring Anschutz's offer to the board. He was offering 40 percent over the current stock price.

One of the board members said: "We can't say 'no' unless you can show us how the return to shareholders can be more than 40 percent over today's share price." I tried my best to lay out the coming years, but of course I could not absolutely guarantee a 40 percent premium over the current stock price. Nobody could guarantee something like that.

We voted on the offer and it was 6 to 3. The nays were Julius, Dick and me. I knew that if Qwest bought us, it would be the end of what we had built at LCI. I knew that Nacchio and Anschutz were all about the numbers. They didn't care about the fundamentals of LCI and the kind of corporate culture and structure that we had worked so hard to build. For me, there was more to LCI than money.

My ultimate fiduciary responsibility was to the stockholders, so we finally agreed unanimously to sell LCI to Qwest. I had Joe Lawrence (who was now my CFO, finally joining us in '95) and Doug Karp negotiate the nitty-gritty of the sale, partly because I didn't have the heart to do it. Because of all my equity, people came to me and said, "Brian, you're going to be rich." True, and board members who weren't already millionaires became so as did the executive group, about 23 of them. Some of them immediately retired to Florida. I couldn't get many of them to go out and do anything after that, but that wasn't me. One of the terms I insisted upon was that the executives would receive a severance if removed by the company within a year. Or, they could stay on for a year at their current compensation. My goal was to maintain their input into the company.

The other term I wanted for me was to be on the board of Qwest. This was not negotiable because I wanted to make sure that my people were treated properly in the new structure and that the integration of the companies maintained some semblance of their value because I was a reasonably good-sized owner and so were many other LCI investors. I told Phil: 'I'll be happy to take on the CEO role, but if you want someone else that's fine, too. But you should find someone other than Joe Nacchio because he can't run this company.' I had no faith in him, considering his experience and temperament.

Phil insisted that Joe stay, and asked that I be vice-chairman so I could keep an eye on the company as best as I could. Unfortunately, Joe was CEO and there was nothing I could do about it. One of the first things I suggested to him was that they keep the racing program. It was a winning proposition, but he and his coterie didn't like racing. Whether they liked racing or not should have been beside the point. The program brought in revenue way beyond what it cost. 'I don't know how you can deny the dollars and cents of it,' I told Joe, but he and his head of marketing were adamant that the racing program was over. The head of marketing was a young guy who Joe put on the staff because his father had worked with Joe at AT&T. It was classic AT&T cronyism, plus Joe wanted to hurt AT&T because they fired him He wanted to hire him and others away from AT&T and gave them big jobs.

My friend Roger Penske picked up our driver Andre Ribeiro as well as Gil de Ferren, with whom we had a minor sponsorship, and subsequently added Indy Lite champion Hélio Castroneves. He went on to win three Indy 500 races for Roger. Many more people know him now as a winner on *Dancing with the Stars.*

Interestingly, Joe Lawrence stayed on, and Phil kept asking him to be COO but he wouldn't do it because he didn't want to work that closely with Nacchio. He stuck around for a year before throwing in the towel. A few other people stayed on, too, but the company began deteriorating. The fundamentals were crumbling, but Wall Street was caught up in a telecom/high tech frenzy, and the share price kept rising.

I wanted to distance myself from all of this because I felt that it would end badly. I hung on only because the stock price seemed to be holding even though I knew that it was artificially inflated like the rest of the market.

After six months I left the board, but I didn't cash out my stock. I should have, but I didn't and it was a mistake. I lost about $100 million, but my loyalties ran deep. Roy Wilkins, who I knew from Williams Communications and my days in Tulsa, resigned from the board around the same time that I did. We both felt that Nacchio was misleading the board regarding their financial situation and product uniqueness. Even more importantly, we were suspicious that he was improperly using classified government contracts to make up for quarter-end shortfalls.

Even though I was no longer a board member, Phil came to me and asked my opinion about buying U.S. West, one of the larger regional Bell Operating Companies. I said: 'Hell, you bought me; you might as well keep going. At least with U.S. West you'll put a floor under the company's equity price because they've got a guaranteed monopoly. So, that's probably a fail-safe acquisition.'

They went ahead with the purchase, but Nacchio ended up alienating everyone at U.S. West, just like he did at LCI and, unfortunately, dissipated both assets. His problem stemmed from how he treated people at both acquired companies. He also never moved out of New Jersey to be at the companies, something that I believe a leader should do. He had the board supply him a plane so he could commute. There wasn't anything I could do, and I remember fielding calls from people who had been at LCI asking me for help, but I had no sway.

Eventually, Qwest ran up huge debts and was forced to sell out to another company. Nacchio was sentenced to six years for insider trading of Qwest stock. I had a similar experience with losing money on MCI stock. In September, 1998, Bert Roberts sold MCI to WorldCom, a much smaller regional long distance company in Jackson, Mississippi. WorldCom was headed by Bernie Ebbers, who showed his notorious side early on. So much so that when Bernie bought MCI, Jerry Taylor immediately sold all of his MCI shares because he didn't trust Bernie. It stemmed from an instance when WorldCom owed MCI about $100 million for interconnections, and they weren't paying their bills. Bernie was shuffling money around, and Jerry was tired of chasing him for payment. Finally, Jerry said that if WorldCom didn't pay its bill within 48 hours, their network connections would be severed. Bernie cursed at Jerry and dared him to shut them down. Jerry did, and two hours later the owed money showed up in MCI's bank account. WorldCom had the money but was playing fast and loose with vendors. In fact, one of the reasons Bernie bought MCI was to avoid making some of these payments. There may have been a hint of revenge in there, too.

What happened to the combined company, now called MCIWorldcom, became legendary. Bernie had so overextended the company as the stock was declining that he was in a real fix. He began receiving pressure from banks to cover margin calls on his stock that was used to finance other businesses like timber and yachting. He was forced to sell stock, which made the price drop even lower. The company was in a tailspin.

Bernie just didn't make poor business choices, he also ran very close to the edge of the law. It turned out that WorldCom was booking interconnection expenses with other telecommunications companies as capital instead of expenses on the balance sheet. They also inflated revenues with bogus accounting entries from what he termed 'corporate unallocated revenue accounts.' A few years later, an audit showed that the company had inflated assets by $11 billion. It became one of the largest corporate scandals in American business history. The stock was worthless and I lost $60 million on paper. Again, I held the stock partly out of loyalty to a company (and its people) that I had helped build into a premier telecommunications company only to watch it disappear because of deception and mismanagement. Eventually, Bernie Ebbers was found guilty of fraud, conspiracy and filing false documents with regulators. He was sentenced to 25 years in prison.

Money wasn't the only issue for me. Certainly I had done well with the sale of LCI, but these companies were more to me than that. I believed that there was almost no limit to where LCI could have gone. It could have become the leading telecommunications company in the United States and perhaps the world. MCI fell apart because of mismanagement, and it, too, could have grown and continued to be one of the world's premier telecommunications companies.

To me, it was more about the fundamentals than cashing out. Are you building a company? Are you taking the long view, one of my red thread strands? Are you building lasting value for shareholders? For the people who invest with you, can you build something of value? Can you create opportunities for all of your employees to do things that they never thought they could do? Can you be a part of the real American corporate infrastructure, which I still contend is overloaded with good people despite what many in the public think about corporate leaders?

It's too easy to become cynical because of companies like World-Com and people at other companies achieving positions that had nothing to do with their ability to manage. When you look at how some people are rewarded for managing, quite often it's not for doing a good job. Most times it is, but it's the 'most times' that people don't look at. They focus on the flameouts. They like to hear about the crooks. They like to hear that there aren't American business heroes anymore except for the celebrity CEOs who many folks assume cheat their way to the top.

I'd like to believe that I am part of a group of leaders who are solid, forthright CEOs. Roger Penske is like that and so are many others. It comes down to ethical behavior, another red thread strand, that's driven by a moral compass but also by fundamentals of believing that what you're doing is right and honest and getting your people to believe it, too. Running a business is not easy, and running a well-thought-of and successful business is even harder, and it comes from the top.

———

Chapter 11

Dublin Calling

Before LCI was sold, while the company was still growing rapidly, I was able to honor my Irish heritage by getting involved in an advisory panel whose aim was to move Ireland forward economically. Through people I knew much earlier during my time at MCI, I was introduced to Donald Keough, who had been president at Coca-Cola. Even though he was no longer at the company - he had worked there for more than 25 years - he was very much involved as what you might call a 'father confessor' to many people who were still there. Don knew everyone. He even was best friends with Warren Buffett before Buffett had made huge investments in Coca-Cola. They met when they were both young fathers in Omaha living across the street from each trying to get their business careers started.

One day Don phoned me. "We're going to put together a group of people who have multiple disciplines. They're all friends of mine and Ireland." At the time, Don had become chairman of Allen & Company, a unique investment banking firm in New York. "I've been working with the prime minister of Ireland, and he's asked me to put together an advisory group." Don explained that the prime minister wanted to build relationships with the Irish-American community not only because it was large but because there was a great deal of business expertise there that he wanted to tap.

The first group that Donald had put together included Jack Welch of General Electric and Tony O'Reilly who ran Heinz in Pittsburgh. Others included Phil Geier head of WPP, Brian Burns, a lawyer from San Francisco, Dan Rooney, owner of the Pittsburgh Steelers, Dan Tully, CEO of Merrill Lynch, Walter O'Hara, a partner in Allen & Co., Denis Kelleher, who built Wall Street Access, Tom Moran, who runs Mutual of America, Bill Connell of Connell Limited Partnership in Boston and John Canning of Madison Dearborn Partners. The group became the *Irish-American Economic Advisory Committee* and we visited prime minister Albert Reynolds in October 1994.

We spent a week touring, talking and listening. We started in Shannon and worked our way to Dublin visiting companies and universities to learn about current economic projects and conditions.

One highly emotional moment during our trip occurred at a private restaurant that the prime minister favored. We had all arrived on time and waited for PM Reynolds who was late. Once there, he began speaking. Tears filled his eyes. He had just received a call from IRA officials in Belfast, telling him that they had agreed to put their weapons down. It was the beginning of an armistice. It was not a peace accord, but it was a huge move in the right direction for that part of the island that had been in conflict for so long.

As we discussed among ourselves the tour we had just finished, we were struck in particular by what we had heard from graduating MBA students. They wanted us to understand their frustration with the Irish economy. They couldn't start a company in Ireland because there was no venture money. Even if they could, by some miracle or good fortune start a company, the firm would have to pay a 40 percent tax on earnings. At the same time, the government was offering a 10 percent corporate tax rate to foreign companies investing in the country. These graduates would probably take their MBAs and work in London or Boston instead. Some would work for foreign companies investing *in* Ireland. To them and to us, it was a nonsensical situation.

The group continued operating and we formed an economic advisory group headed by Donald, which would meet with the prime minister on a regular basis either in Ireland, New York or Washington during the St. Patrick's Day visit of the *Taoiseach*, the Gaelic word for Prime Minister. We came up with many ideas and thoughts about changes that should be made including tax revision. I considered myself the black sheep of the group because I harped about the importance of one item – telecommunications. I kept telling the prime minister and anyone else who would listen that the country needed competition. Telecommunications was a monopoly, prices were too high, and the service was questionable. There appeared to be no incentive by anybody to change the situation. During the time I was involved with the group, we went through several prime ministers. Albert Reynolds stepped down, and John Bruton replaced him. He was there for a short time before Bertie Ahern took his place. Every chance I had, I explained to each of them about the importance of competitive telecommunications if the Irish economy was to become world class.

In the meantime, another group with which I was involved, the Global Information Infrastructure Commission, was trying to move the European Community towards competitive telecommunications. The GIIC was organized and led by Diana Lady Dougan who had been in several U.S. administrations as Ambassador responsible for telecom relationships in the State Department. She had pulled together for the GIIC a group comprised of about 45 CEOs worldwide who were interested in the future of telecommunications infrastructure because we knew that wireless was coming and that data networks would play a major role.

The GIIC managed to get the World Trade Organization, as well as the International Telecommunications Union in Geneva, to take the position that competition was vital for economic growth. They agreed that it was crucial for all ITU member countries to begin introducing competition. This was a breakthrough.

The European Union finally adopted the notion that telecommunications competition was the future, and they gave

EU nations three threshold dates to begin changing their infrastructure from one owned by the government to one run by private companies. The dates were 1996, 1998, and 2002, and the idea was to give some smaller countries a little more time if they felt it was in their best interests to transition more slowly.

Unfortunately for our Irish advisory group, there were political pressures inside the country to take the maximum time, until 2002, to change over. I had no choice but to harangue the prime minister, somewhat unmercifully, I must admit. 'You are going to be left behind as a nation because everybody else is going to adopt this,' I said. 'Their costs for communication are going to drop, and everybody's going to want to invest in these countries instead of yours. This is not a place you want to be.'

My insistence must have worked because in the spring of 1998 I received a call from Brendan Tuohy, Assistant Secretary, Department of Public Enterprise. He said that they had recommended to privatize the telephone infrastructure. He and others in his department wanted to visit me at LCI, along with other telecom companies, so we could brief them on how competitive telecom worked.

I was halfway through my presentation, during a break, when Brendan said: "Mr. Thompson, could we let the staff continue with this meeting so you and I can talk privately in your office?"

Once alone, he said: "Let me tell you the real reason I'm here. We've got a problem. I understand that you've been talking about this for a long time with our prime minister, and I have been directed to see if you could help us sort out the issue. What you've been saying has come to pass. Microsoft has been producing software in Ireland, shrink wrapping and then shipping, but now they want to start sending their software over the telecom network instead. They believe that network costs are too high in Ireland and are considering moving their plant to the continent where telecommunications costs are lower. We're hearing the same sorts of things out of chip maker Intel - that Ireland's telecom costs are too high. The country would lose a lot of money if these companies move their plants out of Ireland."

'That's pretty heavy stuff,' I said. I offered to make some calls and see if I could pull together an advisory group or committee to do a quick analysis of the situation and come up with some answers.

One of the first people I called was Ray Smith, who I knew from my days at MCI when I ran the Mid-Atlantic division and he headed the regional Bell company. I always respected him, even though we often were on opposite sides of the table. Other members were Don Heath, who had worked for MCI in data communications and was head of the Internet Society, a group that promotes equal access to the Internet. Next was Vint Cerf, who, of course, spearheaded MCI's data network efforts and now is considered one of the 'fathers of the Internet.' There was Diana Dougan, at GIIC, a natural for the group, and Doug Karp, a Warburg Pincus partner who was incredibly sharp on telecom financing. He was on my LCI board and one of the smartest guys I knew in the investment community. Finally, I tapped Denis Gilhooly, an excellent writer on telecommunications and technology, who was an advisor on information infrastructure to the World Bank and founder of *Telecommunications Week International*. He would also be integral in helping us to prepare all of our reports.

We also had four Irish nationals on the committee including Brendan who I had asked to line up all the key players in Ireland: Telecom Eireann, which was the Irish telephone company, Sat, which was a new competitor, the existing government policy makers and all of the major user groups. We set up two full days of presentations and discussions. Our first meeting was in June, and as I looked around the U-shaped table there was Diana tapping away on her laptop as were Vint and Ray and Don. I was sitting next to Doug, and we just had pen and paper. Laptops were still fairly new. During the first break I said, 'What are you doing over there, Vint?' He said, "Oh, I was just writing an outline for the final report." And Diana said, "You know, I was doing something similar, but I was fleshing out our job charter." Ray said: "I was just taking notes on what the presenters were saying." There was no such thing as Wi-Fi at the time, so halfway through the first day, they swapped floppy disks, and I realized that we had chosen the perfect group of people.

At the end of the first day we had an outline of our report. The second meeting was in late August, and our conclusion was that Ireland was isolated and depended upon connectivity to London for all its telecommunications. Part of it was technical but there was a political facet, too. We proposed that they build a direct fiber link from Dublin to the U.S., which then would connect to the rest of the world - without having to go through London.

By the time we were finished with the second series of meetings I had already called in two other CEOs from big firms doing business in Europe: Global Crossing, a roll-up of several carriers engaged in transatlantic fiber networks, and FLAG, partially owned by NYNEX - one of the regional Bell companies - which stood for Fiber Link Around the Globe. Their network went from Singapore to London and they were trying to go across the Atlantic but hadn't yet accomplished it.

Brendan took on the job of negotiating with these carriers and within two months he had a commitment from Global Crossing to bring a fiber, on a spur, directly from their transatlantic fiber into Dublin. This happened even before we issued our final report in December, which had only ten recommendations related to building competition. For me, professionally, it was a culmination of all the consulting jobs I had done. The report was clear, succinct and simple.

The Dail, or Irish Parliament, responded rapidly to our efforts, allowing competition through a regulatory approach and supporting the steps we recommended. Ireland already had some competition, but it was just reselling private line service. This vote told the rest of the world that they were serious about encouraging true competition. As proof of their commitment, the government was planning to sell their ownership in the national telephone company. They also promised to bring high capacity digital technology directly to Dublin by using Global Crossing's facilities.

When we were finished with our work, the minister called me. "I would like you to join the board of Telecom Eireann."

'No, I don't think so,' I replied. 'I apologize for being blunt, but it's a board of purely political appointees. They have nothing to add. They don't truly understand telecom. The CEO of the company seems very arrogant, and the unions are obstructionists. If I can't be effective in doing something I'm not going to do it.'

She understood, but between Christmas and New Year's she called again. "Brian, I took what you said to heart. I took your advice; I just fired the whole board. It will be made public in a few hours, and I would like you to become chairman."

What could I say now? How could I say 'no,' especially because I had just resigned from the board of Qwest? I agreed to become the non-executive chairman of Telecom Eireann, which was in the process of taking the company public, removing it from government control. They were becoming a publicly-owned company run by an elected board with the responsibility of being the largest carrier in the country. To ensure that they weren't going to abuse the competition, they had to sell their cable TV business. They also operated a wireless service, which we didn't jettison at the time but made it clear that we were going to operate in a competitive manner.

I was upfront with the minister and the board about my role. I was still interested in seeking a CEO position at another company, but I would make certain there would not be a conflict with being at Telecom Eireann.

This was my intention, but I got blindsided.

Adam Solomon, the person who had gotten me involved with LCI, but had since left Warburg Pincus, called me about an opportunity. "Brian, I've got this other board I'm on, and we're building a fiber network throughout Europe, and we have a partnership with all the railroads. This is the next MCI."

I listened as he laid out the deal. Then I said: 'One of the things you've got to assure me is that they don't have any interests in Ireland. I can't have a conflict with my position at Telecom Eireann.'

"There's nothing in Ireland, so it's not a problem," he said.

'No intention of being in Ireland, nothing on the horizon?' I wanted to be certain.

"Nothing," he promised.

He wanted me to take over the reins at GTS, Global Tele-Systems, which was composed of scattered European telecom carriers hoping one day to become a global player. The current head was Jerry Thames, who had been knocking around the telecommunications landscape including a stint at British Telecom where he was head of data communications. At the time, GTS was doing about $300 or $400 million worth of business after starting as an enterprise known as the San Francisco-Moscow Teleport, a not-for-profit carrier which had built in the early 1990s a communications link between the United States and the Soviet Union in order to promote peaceful relations. It was a well-meaning project.

The Teleport's seed money had come from George Soros and a New York investor named Alan Slifka. The project was doing pretty well financially, even though it was just a link between San Francisco and Moscow. Because they had a monopoly to interconnect networks, they produced a large cash flow and now wanted to expand beyond Moscow. Their approach was to become part of a larger project called *Hermes* which was to build a fiber network along European railroads' rights of way. They received their first round of investments, beyond the San Francisco-Moscow Teleport, and now were no longer a not-for-profit organization.

The board wanted Thames to step down because they weren't happy with his performance. We negotiated for months and finally hammered out a deal. I called the Irish minister to tell her that I was close to consummating a deal with GTS, which legally was a U.S. company operating out of Northern Virginia and London. My plan was to have a COO work out of London while I stayed in Northern Virginia, which was where Thames also had been stationed. When I told the minister about my plans, she was very happy for me.

The day before we were going to announce my new position, the minister called me with some bad news. "Mr. Thompson, I have an invitation on my desk to be at the opening of the GTS office in Dublin next Tuesday."

I was shocked. How could this have happened even after I had been reassured for months that there would not be any GTS business done in Ireland? It turned out that before he was to step down, Thames had acquired a small group of new competitors including one in Dublin, apparently initiated on his own without fully consulting the board. I was livid and got the board to agree that they would withdraw their plans to open shop in Ireland but it was too late. The newspapers had already printed news of the office opening and if the company changed plans, it would have made the minister look bad. The political fallout would have been unmanageable.

Reluctantly, I had to quit my position as chairman of Telecom Eireann, and it foretold even more trouble ahead.

The second indication that I was heading into rough seas was when I learned that just a week before I signed on they had told me, only indirectly, that they had agreed to buy a French company for $400 million. It was another one of Thames' bad ideas. His plan was to trim payrolls to make the acquisition viable, but he either didn't know or didn't take into consideration the social laws of France that make it difficult to fire employees.

Adding to the company's problems was that the fiber network was a mish-mash – four fibers over here, eight over there – a crazy quilt stitched together. Another issue was that in return for their rights of way, the railroads owned a large portion of the company through stock. Some of the shareholders wanted to stay, and some wanted out, so we were never sure where we stood.

Organizationally, it was a mess. The actual operation of the network was taking place in Brussels, but the decisions on running the infrastructure came from London. We also had offices in Sweden, Norway, Germany and elsewhere that were reselling network capacity to other carriers. We had bought resellers, including one in Germany, to which we were trying to connect. In order to serve them quickly, we had leased facilities. As I tipped over the stones, there were more worms underneath. Sometimes a whole bunch of worms. Thames had not done adequate due diligence on any of the company's acquisitions. He rushed them through the board trying to move rapidly, counting on the frenzy still surrounding investors' interest in telecom. He seemed to have the attitude: "Hey, money is free. We'll buy it now and sort it out later."

Unfortunately, I was the person who had to sort it all out.

There was a board member named Bob Amman who I had met through Ben LeBow from the Western Union deal that we had done at MCI. I didn't know him all that well but enough to feel comfortable with him. He was a hale fellow well met, decent sort of a guy. I told Bob that I was not going to live in London, but that I might send him there as COO if he was interested. He had operating experience and understood what I was trying to accomplish. He said he would be willing to move to London, and I thought this would be an excellent move for him and the company.

Well, it turned out to be a mistake. He was one of those guys who throws himself into an office and then tries to do things, but he wasn't really an operations person after all. I had trusted him, but he simply didn't get done what I had asked of him. He would have meetings, but nothing would be accomplished. He turned out to be a bureaucrat and not a manager. His background was corporate politics, not corporate teamwork.

I guess I was fooled, but you never know how someone is going to operate until they actually try to run something on their own. I had never worked with him in a situation like the one he was currently in. I had admired his level-headedness and patience, but I should have seen the early warning signs when he rented a house that cost us $5,000 a month to lease - and that appeared to be more important to him than running the business. In addition, his wife had a fairly lavish lifestyle in this new setting. When it comes to leading companies, I'm not very much for trappings of power, and I had hoped that he felt the same way. Apparently, he didn't.

I told Bob that we were not able to raise any more money and had to cut our expenses. I said that I was going to tell this to the board, and I needed him to back me up. He agreed but when we got into the meeting, he announced: "I know nothing about this," and then accused me of being an absentee manager in London. It was a classic case of political self-dealing.

The board wanted to borrow more money to install additional underground fiber. I countered that we had enough because we now employed the latest technology to light a single fiber with a terabyte of capacity. 'We don't need any more,' I told them. 'We have enough fiber, we just need the salespeople to sell what we have. And the financial markets seem to have closed on us.'

The company was unraveling. Our people in France were telling me that their situation was a disaster. People were leaving and, unfortunately, not those we would have liked to leave. We went from 400 to 160 employees, and some were starting their own companies.

I decided amid all of this chaos that Bob had to go. I was in the process of firing him and told him that he had to find something else. He said he was fine with leaving, that he would even help me find a successor. We started interviewing people. At the same time, he was continuing to work behind my back, telling the board that I was the real problem and not him – but I didn't know any of this. One of the people that Bob and I interviewed was Duncan Lewis who was at Cable & Wireless. We were going through the process of moving out Bob and replacing him with Duncan. Or so I thought.

It took me six months to unearth all of these problems, and it was a painful experience trying to work my way out of it. I thought I had done my due diligence, but once I was in the company I found myself waltzing into something that I didn't expect. I wasn't able to get the support I needed to succeed, and I only lasted 18 months.

Once I left, Bob became the CEO and Duncan was the COO. They rode off into the sunset and into bankruptcy 11 months later. With them went my own personal financial investment in the company of about $20 million.

The story becomes even more horrible for me personally. I had asked Jeff Von Deylen, who was my controller at LCI, a man I liked and trusted, to go to Europe to keep an eye on the financial side of the operation. I thought he would have my back, but I was wrong. Amman got him into a position where he believed he would be the next CFO of the company, and he worked against me. The company was toxic, and my shortcoming was that I had counted on people's loyalty. To me, loyalty, trust, and openness are critical to a company's success.

Ironically, just as I was leaving, I was in the midst of selling the company to a partnership of GTE and Verizon which would have solved our money problems. As we reached the end of negotiations, and I was on my way out of the company, the final decision to merge became Bob's and he didn't follow up. Would the partnership have bought GTS and saved the company? Who knows? It was a 50/50 chance, but we'll never know.

Now here's the strangest part of all this. When I was still vice chairman of Qwest, I was trying to convince Joe Nacchio about the value of international relationships. I thought that even though LCI was now part of Qwest, I could still keep them on the right track so the company could be a player in international telecommunications. I took Joe to Europe to introduce him to some of the telecom company officials that I knew. Again, I should have realized that Nacchio was trying to emulate how AT&T went about business when he took a tony suite at the Dorchester hotel, and I insisted on a regular room. Anyway, I introduced him to the people at KPN, which was a telecom provider in The Netherlands. Eventually, they negotiated a deal for a new company named KPNQwest. The goal was to unite the two companies' fiber expertise and continue to expand the network in Europe. So, when GTS went bankrupt, and the board was looking for someone to buy them, along came Nacchio and KPNQwest to buy GTS. Looking back, I'm sure that Von Deylen had a hand in this.

In 2002 – I had already been gone for two years - KPNQwest collapsed about six months after acquiring GTS. The collapse was largely due to the dotcom boom which had inflated the worth of telecom companies and could not be sustained. Many companies had done 'hollow swaps' with each other creating artificial revenue figures and incorrect financial guidance. The collapse was even more dramatic than other failures because two years earlier KPNQwest was estimated to be carrying more than half of Europe's IP traffic.

In hindsight, perhaps I was naïve to believe that what I had been able to do at LCI and MCI could be applied to GTS because it was the next opportunity that presented itself to me. What other lessons did I learn from this experience? One of them was that I was too full of myself to listen to logic. My wife disliked the board very much, and that should have been a tip off, but I figured I could handle them. I also was impressed that George Soros was represented on the board and we would be associated. It was arrogance on my part.

The real sorrow for me was that I had to leave my position as non-executive chairman of Telecom Eireann where I really could have made a difference. Just before I left Telecom Eireann, I was trying to talk the minister out of her idea to aggressively sell the company's shares broadly to the Irish public. I implored her at our last meeting: 'You don't want to do this; telecoms are at such a high share price right now that you want the institutions buying in, and not the public. This is IPO material. If prices fall, and they probably will, the public will be really angry with you.' She insisted on wanting Irish citizens to make money on the IPO like the all the 'fat cats' had in the past. Sadly, many people lost their life savings.

The whole thing went south, and they ended up being bought out by Providence Partners and Tony O'Reilly as part of a private equity group that went in and stripped assets to sustain budgets and pay investors healthy fees and dividends and take it public once again. While private investors made more than four times their money in a short period, they left a fairly hollow company facing massive challenges.

It was a tough time for the telecom industry and for me person-ally. I was licking my wounds wondering what to do next. Did I act too impulsively and arrogantly or was I a victim of bad luck and unscrupulous people? I had some soul-searching to do.

Still, I moved forward.

I decided to reenergize a company - Universal Telecommunica-tions, Inc. - that I had started in the early 1990s after I left MCI and use it as vehicle for personal investments for my family. I decided to lend the company money and make my two children each a 20 percent partner, and I would hold 60 percent. I would do some investments and deals using the company as a platform and see how things went. As usual, I was looking for my next gig.

I had no idea that my next venture would bring me almost full circle to a client that I had worked with decades earlier at McKinsey.

———

Chapter 12

Building A Company To Last

As I left GTS, I got a call from Jeff Ganek who had worked for me at MCI and then at GTS (before my involvement) with a stopover in between at GTE's Spacenet. Now, he was at a division of Lockheed in the area of information technologies working with a fellow named John Brophy, and the two of them were putting together a number portability business. Telephone companies were going to be required to allow customers to keep their phone numbers wherever they moved, even outside of their area codes. Jeff and John were working on a system that would keep track of everybody's phone number so calls could be seamlessly forwarded to them.

Jeff was the lead person, and John, his boss, was the creative business mind who I also considered an entrepreneur inside a large corporation, a subject in which I was always interested. But he was also a good politician. He had been with Lockheed for a long time and knew the chairman and all the upper management and got them to agree to fund his projects. One of his successes was putting together what's now known as *E-Z Pass*, which allows us to zip through tolls by paying through a box on our windshields. He also developed databases using sophisticated data manipulation to help track down deadbeat parents.

Jeff introduced me to John. "I've got a problem," John admitted. "Some of the people in top management are trying to get Lockheed to buy COMSAT, and I know that you're familiar with the company." I told him that I had read about this effort in the newspapers, and it was a crazy idea because COMSAT was formed by an act of Congress and the only way it could be sold is by another act of Congress, which was a slim bet. Brophy said that they knew all of this, but Lockheed's upper management still wanted to buy it. They were already almost two years down the road with the acquisition.

Management was committed to the purchase even though they had conflicts of interest because of their number portability business which was a pretty small business at the time, less than $40 million. They needed to sell it before they could buy COMSAT.

I was able to help them sell the number portability business to Warburg Pincus before the purchase of COMSAT took place. There were some internal altercations at Warburg going on at the time, and it was a tense and distracting period, which made the sale more difficult. Doug Karp, the Warburg partner who actually negotiated the sale of LCI for me and was on my board, had decided to leave though he was the major proponent there for the transaction. In any event, Bill Janeway and Henry Kressel moved the acquisition forward and they made what was to become the key investment in their new fund.

I was able to co-invest with Warburg for my role in the sale, about 2 percent of the initial $70 million they put into the company. They owned the company five years before selling it, making about $1.3 billion for their limited partners. Quite a home run. Extricating the company out of Lockheed was a jewel for Jeff and everyone else involved. The spun-off company was named Neustar, the *Neu* stood for *neutral* because they represented all carriers equally, and it's still going strong. Because of their expertise in manipulating large databases, they also were able to handle the allocation of first-level Internet domains like .biz and .us.

After Lockheed bought COMSAT, John said to me: "They really don't know what to do with it. You've got to come and talk to the CEO. Can you help us make some order out of this chaos?"

They had formed a division named Lockheed Global Telecommunications, and COMSAT was one element of it. Eventually, I

talked to Vance Coffman, the CEO, and my advice was to liqui-
date the whole telecom business and get out of it whatever they
could. 'The problem, Vance,' I said, 'is that you paid $2-1/2 billion
for COMSAT, merged it into other telecom assets and everything
together is not worth more than $700 to $800 million.' He was not
pleased to hear my assessment.

Vance got us together with their CFO and we all discussed
the matter in depth. After four or five months, they asked me to
join Lockheed as an executive vice president overseeing this division with the responsibility of tidying it up and getting it properly
divested or, alternatively, properly putting it together. 'I understand what you want me to do,' I said, 'but I don't want to just work
for you. I want our interests and objectives to be aligned.' I suggested that my remuneration be performance-based and in line
with how much I could get for the sale, if that's what they decided
to do. I was trying to convince them that they needed to take a
write-off on these assets, but they didn't want to do it.

They decided later to jettison COMSAT by striking a compro-
mise whereby some assets were sold to other carriers and the direct
retail communications business was all that was left in COMSAT.

A group of investors would take it off their hands for no cash,
assume the liabilities and Lockheed would still own about 20 percent of it. Lockheed had just gotten a big defense department contract for the F-22 jet which put them in a better financial position
to take a COMSAT write-off.

They were putting the finishing touches on the deal when the
investors came to me through Phil Walker, a mutual friend, and
asked me to join them because of my telecom experience and my
previous involvement with COMSAT while I was with McKinsey.
They also knew of my attempt to help Coffman and Lockheed deal
with their business.

I laid out my offer. 'If you want me to be involved I'll be glad
to do so, but I'm not going to be the CEO. I'm not going to take
an active, full-time role in it. I will buy a little piece so I can be an
investor along with you.' I added: 'I'd like you to give me options
toward shares. At some point they might be worth something and

I can give them to my kids through my company UTI, and they'll get some benefit from it. I will be the chairman and work half time so you can give me a pittance of a salary. I'll take the same health care benefits as you and we'll work together in the same office.'

Eventually, we became partners - George Kappaz, Tim Harmon, Phil Walker and me, and I became chairman of COMSAT in 2003.

Together we took COMSAT from virtually nothing to being one of the largest suppliers of telecommunications services in South America and Central America, even though we never owned any satellites. We did buy the IBM network in Central America, which turned out well, and a company in Mexico that was a disaster. We turned COMSAT from a company that had less than $50 million in revenues - and they were losing $7 or $8 million a year on net revenue stream - to about a $260 million company that was making good money.

If you walk the streets of Buenos Aires today, you'll see manholes that say COMSAT because they had installed fiber all around the city. We built satellite-based, government-funded networks in Columbia with about 4,000 points of presence and 9,000 points of presence in Brazil. We built facilities in Sao Paolo, including a large earth station about an hour outside of the city. This facility and the 'social networks' that we built allowed the governments of both countries to take advantage of the growing need for communications and information exchange among the mass population.

I enjoyed this endeavor very much, because there were interesting people coming and going and it was a pleasant place to work. It was also fun to work again with our race car driver Andre and his brother Lincoln, who now was managing a communications company called ATRIUM that was serving Lincoln's father-in-law's real estate businesses in Brazil. They used our communications network some of the time. To me, it was yet another example of how people weave through your life.

It also gave me a breather because I didn't have to work full time. I must admit that it was a kick having a business card that said, 'Chairman of COMSAT.' It was also completion of a full circle for me because of my experience with COMSAT decades earlier.

In 2008 we sold COMSAT to British Telecom for Latin American operations. BT at the time was seeking a presence in Latin America and COMSAT fit into their plans. It was a good exit strategy for us as well.

Before I left COMSAT, though, I was toying with the idea of setting up what was known as a *special purpose acquisition company* in which we were to build a public blind fund for investing purposes. The management team would be responsible for finding deals, bringing them to the investors and asking them to vote in favor of putting their money into the enterprise. I was to be the CEO.

The company was public by virtue of holding an IPO, and the charter outlined who the leaders were, what they were allowed to invest in and so forth. One of the rules was that you could not have a deal in your pocket ready to go. You had to be out there looking for new opportunities. There were two parts to the offering. First was the portion in which you sold stock and warrants, and there were more warrants for every share of stock you sold because that was the money earmarked for walking around and finding deals. The second part had a lot fewer warrants. The overall plan was to raise money and place it in a trust fund which accrued interest at Treasury rates. If, at the end of a specified period, you didn't find anything to invest in, the money went back to the investors.

By the time we finished with our road show we could have raised about $300 million, but I didn't want to use that much money because we would be competing with private equity firms. When you raise over $100 million you enter the realm of private equity firms, and I didn't want to be there, so we raised about $60 million.

That was in April 2004, and we had to find a deal within 18 months to bring to our shareholders for their up or down vote. We would be obligated to send out the proxy statement just as you would for an annual meeting except that in this case the shareholders were voting on a deal. The terms were all public. All of the shareholders had a vote, and if more than 20 percent voted against the deal it collapsed, and you gave everybody back their money except for what was used as expenses. If the deal went ahead, those who voted 'no' would get their money back as long as enough people stayed in.

At the time we were doing this, such investment companies had not been in vogue for about ten years. It had been done in the early 1990s - in fact Rod Hackman was involved in one of these - and they enjoyed reasonable success. I knew Rod when he was at Kidder Peabody in the 1980s; he was their telecom investment banker.

We thought it was the right time to bring this idea back again because many of the venture capitalist funds were not buying anything and small companies still needed funding. The VCs had been hurt by the early 2000's Internet/tech bubble and they had amassed a lot of money, keeping it on the sidelines, but they were not using it.

What we were really offering, at its core, was my reputation, credibility and accomplishments.

Rod had a small boutique investment bank that was called Mercator Partners, and our company was called Mercator Partners Acquisition Corporation, MPAC.

We had studied several opportunities, but one in particular seemed most promising. It grew from a failed deal that was attempting to do a reverse merger of two companies into a shell. We looked at the companies and realized that it made more sense to merge them instead and not have any kind of shell.

One of the companies was GII, which stood for Global Internetworking, Inc., and after I talked with the executives at Rod's suggestion, I thought it was a strong foundation for building a larger company. The company had begun by being a provisioning company for the Bell companies. If Bell Atlantic, for example, was trying to complete a circuit in Louisiana, this company would work with Bell South on behalf of Bell Atlantic. They would do the negotiating, find circuits and generally became a one-stop shopping outsource company. They would resell circuits to the Bell companies and make money on the spread. They made additional money by operating the network for Bell Atlantic and handling the billing. They would enjoy a small margin for their efforts, but it was guaranteed business. Even though they had one-year contracts, most of the time this arrangement carried on for a longer time.

Author (left), Rick Calder, President & CEO, GTT and Chris McKee, General Counsel, GTT discussing a pending acquisition; January 2013.
Author's collection.

This company had a platform called CMD or Customer Management Database, which they built themselves. It was impressive to me because they had gotten together with carriers like Bell Atlantic, which by that time changed its name to Verizon, and others, and established electronic interfaces with them. Because of GII's sophisticated database they could plug in two addresses, one, say in Chicago, and another in Fort Worth, and they could generate the availability and the cost of connecting a customer through different carriers, time of day, connection type ... everything. Their software did all the calculations for customers and would give them the best deal.

The other company was ETT, European Telecom and Technology. They built a business by pitching large telecom users and saying: "We can connect your Volvo plants and your Jaguar plants and your Land Rover plants together into your network that terminates here in London, and we can do it a lot cheaper than British Telecom. We'll do all the negotiations in whatever country is necessary. We'll take on all the headaches. We'll coordinate the network and we'll build it for you."

About 75 to 80 percent of their business was with private enterprises, so they were in a completely different part of the market than GII in the United States, but what they did was similar. As I studied their business, I was taken aback that they were doing most of their recordkeeping on spreadsheets and would bill customers manually at month's end. They had some computer billing, but it wasn't fully integrated. The sales head kept much of the billing records in his desk drawer.

It was a simple business model but unique in that nobody else was willing to do the transnational networking, which was a pain because of all the different governments and jurisdictions. We had started to do that at GTS before the company disappeared, so I knew what was involved and it wasn't easy. They would also take on service level agreements, which meant that even though they were only a reseller, they guaranteed a certain level of performance. This was a plus when you were trying to sell your service to large companies because they insisted on reliability.

When I looked at the European company and compared it to the U.S. company, I thought it would be a good fit because ETT could go into Africa and the Far East and they could integrate with other carriers much more so than the U.S. company. The company here was more U.S.-centric, and seldom went internationally. Together they could be a global telecom provider if we could combine and manage them in concert taking the best traits of both companies. There was nothing sexy about either business, but they both had an ability to run circles around the big guys. They could beat U.S. competitors because of their sophisticated platform and best the European companies because of their ability to negotiate across borders.

It was against this backdrop that we decided to buy both companies. I figured that the two of them together were doing a little over $40 million, and they were both reasonably profitable. If we could combine them we could make them far more efficient, and expand their growth from what it was at the time. I projected about a 10 or 15 percent growth.

We thought it would take about $40 to $50 million to complete the deals and another $10 to $20 million to buy several of some ten smaller companies we had our sights on in similar business to roll into it. When we brought the final deal to the investor shareholders for their vote, some were concerned that it wasn't just one acquisition. It was about merging two companies and realizing benefits through that combination. This idea was of concern to some investors because it was a little out of the ordinary, or at least not what they expected. We firmly believed, though, that the real value was in merging the two companies.

We started the road show after we put the deal together, and it was very attractive on the face of it. We estimated that within three to five years we could take these two companies, worth about $40 million, and grow them at a reasonable rate to be a $200 or $300 million-dollar company in about four or five years - and maybe as much as a half billion dollar company in ten years.

We announced our intention in September and investors had 60 days in which to decide. What happened next, however, shocked me because I didn't expect it.

As I met people who had invested in our company – and they seemed very interested when they signed up – I found that now they didn't seem so interested. It turned out that they didn't invest in the hopes of being in on whatever deal we were able to present to them but were only in it to park their money. They knew we guaranteed a treasury rate of return. Because of how we structured the company they could sell their warrants in the public marketplace and then vote against the deal. This would give them a return on their capital plus interest which amounted to a small but guaranteed profit. The wise guys who bought the warrants for five cents now were selling them for 50 cents.

I thought I was reasonably sophisticated after all the financial and equity deals I had done and I had looked these guys in the eyes and thought they were really listening to my story about building a company. I thought they understood what we were trying to do and that they wanted to be a part of it. They had lied to me and said things like: "I really like the opportunity." It convinced us that we had a strong investor base but it turned out that they weren't sincere.

I had an inkling that we were in trouble when, during our final road show, I would make a presentation and people would be fidgeting and not paying attention. I would ask if there were any questions and people would pop up and say: "When is the vote?," and "What happens if we vote against it?," and "How quickly will I get my money back if it doesn't go forward?" I started getting this everyplace I was going. I had worked 18 months to present a worthwhile deal to these so-called investors and some 25 year-old hotshot was thinking, "If I can get back the treasury rate plus an additional seven percent when I sell off these warrants, then I'm in fat city." I was fooled and it didn't feel good.

Now, we needed to find investors who really wanted to buy into our concept and keep the vote above the 80 percent mark so we could go ahead with our plans to build a lasting company. We worked like hell to find a strategic investor who was interested in doing more than just parking money. It was a struggle. We got the investment bankers to forego some of their costs. That helped. We also got people who were bent on selling shares to sell at slight discounts so that they could get out fast and let us move on.

It was another one of those times when you thought you had the right thing going and were really pleased about everything. It also was one of those times when I thought, "What the hell have I gotten myself into?" We were all close to saying, "Tank the whole thing," but in the last 24 hours we got enough shares committed to move forward with the deal.

We ended up having to return $10 million to the shareholders who wanted their money back. This left us just enough cash to buy the two companies and about $3 million left for working capital. That was it. We had no dry powder left. It was all gone, and we still had to build the new company.

We took the *G* from *Global* from the U.S. company. Then we took the *TT* from the European company and ended up with

Global Telecom and Technology. Mike Keenan, former CEO of GII, was to be the first CEO, and I became executive chairman.

We built a strong board. Rod Hackman, Mike Keenan, Morgan O'Brien, co-founder of Nextel and its chairman. We also had Alex Mandl, former AT&T president, Howard Janzen, former chairman of Williams Communications, Sudhakar Shenoy, chairman and CEO of Information Management Consulting, Inc., and Didier Delepine, president and CEO of Equant N.V.

Unfortunately, I learned after two months that Mike's management style wasn't consistent with our business, so we parted ways. He's still a large shareholder. I would have to take the reins for the next five months, something that I didn't want to do.

Fortunately, we were able to find several key executives willing to take the risk with us including Rick Calder, the current president and CEO. Rick started at MCI, and then worked for Rick Ellenberger at Broadwing Corporation. Before that he worked for Nate Kantor at Winstar. Winstar was one of the very first fixed base wireless companies in the country. Both Ellenberger and Kantor worked with me at MCI.

Windstar was a competitor of Teligent, which was Alex Mandl's company. The two of them started at the same time. They were the progenitors of what is now called Clearwire. Rick Calder's dad was in the U.S. intelligence services so he grew up all over the world. He went to Yale and Harvard Business School. I caught him on the rebound from a company where he was promised a CEO position, but that didn't happen when the CEO decided to stay on. Rick left.

I have coached and pushed and huddled and gone through lots of trials with him, and I've got another few things I want to impart to him before he's really the guy who's going to be there when I won't have to come into the office anymore. He respects that mentoring, which is something a lot of people lack these days.

Other people have been instrumental, including our general counsel Chris McKee, John Hendler and Eric Swank who had left after three years to pursue a start-up.

The company went through a few tough years but was holding its own. We grew through acquisitions and in doing so picked up customer bases. That was our fundamental approach. We could put the acquired company's customers on to our platform with great efficiency. We paid them for that base and kept them and their salespeople as agents to service customers. There was no need for us to go out and hire a big sales force. The agents received an annuity as long as their customer stayed on our network. Aside from the acquisitions, it didn't cost us much to maintain the new customers except for the incremental cost of billing, bad debt and whatever else came along. When I explained our approach to investors, the question often arose: "Is that organic growth?" because that's what investors like to see in companies. 'Yes, we've got organic growth,' was my answer. 'It's not 20 percent, but we can achieve that level of growth by simply acquiring customer bases, bringing them onto our platform and going forward with them.' For us, the total, in essence, is organic growth except we acquire the customers several at a time rather than one by one.

That's not all we were doing. We also upgraded our network technology. We had taken on some networks that were at risk but the risks were small, and it allowed us to increase our market reach.

The good news was that we had gone through the most difficult economic time in the history of our business, of many businesses for the last seven years, and we held our own. We not only held our own but improved our efficiency and the ability for this platform of ours to function. We did everything on the platform. We did all our billing on it; we did all of our customer identification; we have all of our contracts on it; we've got all of our provisioning, all of the order entry, all of the orders themselves. Everything was there and segmented so that the right people had access when they needed it. Our customers in Europe were migrated to our network making it a more efficient operation than ever. Our European people were selling to carriers and intermediaries.

I explained to investors that our company had a simple concept: We were a network integrator that was independent of any underlying network, and we operated on behalf of the customer to get the best deal and to manage it on their behalf. We did all the work so that they didn't need their own telecom staff, or, in some cases, we were the logical extension of their telecom department.

Indeed, today we may be the world's largest interconnected company given our IP and data connections and our more than 600 partners. We are focused on becoming the premier cloud network provider to the world.

It was that simple to get here.

———

One of the beautiful facets of this business is that we've got the most scalable platform you can imagine because all it takes is small, incremental software editions to accommodate new customers. We can take a company that is marginal or not making any money, bring them on and enjoy the synergies. We're not like companies that have to expand to a new market to make more money. We don't have to add a lot of equipment, hire more salespeople. We don't have to do any of that to grow.

One issue, though, is that there is a normal churn rate of two, two-and-a-half percent that takes place because of customers relocating, people moving in and out of business and so forth. We always have to be mindful of that issue.

I give all the credit to our people. We've got a team that understands what they're going to do; we've got a team who's now gotten past living hand to mouth. They went through the valley of the shadow of death. They understand what that is, and it's a place they don't want to be anymore. We've got a group that's steeled.

A fascinating side note is that at MCI and LCI many employees were driven by the stock price as they watched it appreciate. Here, nobody watches it because it's 'trading by appointment only,' and it'll go up and down 20 percent with 200 shares traded, and so until we get to the point where we have a lot of fungibility in the stock, appreciation is not an issue. I'd like to use stock to do some of our acquisitions, but we can't do it at these low prices. We're about $2.50 a share and very thinly traded. Getting analysts to follow us is a challenge that we have not yet conquered.

We have about 18 million outstanding shares, of which 2 million are in options, so there's about 16 million tradable stock out there. I own about 5 million shares, but I didn't have them at the onset. I bought them along the way. The original investors, the ones who got out, bought it for $5 and sold it for about 50 cents at one point. That was unfortunate but a reflection of the time and not our business. We have done just what we said we would do, but it has taken longer because of the $10 million 'surprise' at closing.

Where's our bumble bee? What can sting us when we're least expecting it? The only thing is finding the best people to help us grow. It's not always easy to find people who are oriented to doing the right thing, getting the job done correctly and enjoying solving problems for a customer.

I have no doubt that we're building a nucleus that can become a half-billion dollar company at some point, maybe in three to five years. We will be able, in the next year, to get the investment community to show an interest in us because we'll be bigger than $100 million. We'll probably get some analysts to follow us, and we'll start to get some independent and outside opinions about the company. Sometimes companies become too inwardly focused and lose perspective; having outsiders looking in can be extremely helpful.

That's my hope. I think we're on our way to building a sustainable company not simply for the purpose of cashing out as I have seen so many others around me do but building something that offers employment, self fulfillment to people, that contributes to the community and builds prosperity for the country, especially as we move forward out of our recession.

———

Epilogue

I believe that successful CEOs, more than everything else they must do well, have got to be exceptional complex problem solvers. That's really their fundamental job, so any way that you can get training and experience in solving problems will help you to become an effective CEO and leader.

For me, the ability to solve problems began with my engineering education. The analytical problem-solving that I learned by being an engineer, by going through the training and trying to solve problems technically, created a sense of 'how do I deal with problems; how do I deal with issues that arise?'

From there I went into research - which I didn't want to do at the time - but that helped me greatly, too, because it underscored that I could be creative and analytical at the same time. As I look back, these were two very important factors contributing to my success.

The military undoubtedly was another factor in my business success. It added discipline, the self-discipline that I needed to go forward in business, to be organized as well as analytical in how I approached problems. I joke about it, but my experience in bomb disposal was crucial to my later success. It was a test of my ability to persevere, but also in building my self-confidence. I had to be thoughtful and very methodical about what I did, and not necessarily just in dealing with others, but dealing with myself. As the CEO of a company, you'll end up with three or four 'bombs' being put on your desk every day and you've got to deal with them in a calm and measured way.

Last, Harvard Business School presented me with three or four bombs every day in the form of case studies. I was forced to respond and say 'okay, here are the issues; here is the way I would

173

solve that problem.' The business school experience was very help-ful in giving me both the sense of purpose of business, but also the added self-confidence that I needed because almost all of the people around me were bright and creative. This forced me to step up my game.

My family foundation was critically important, too, because it gave me a sense of how to do things right, to consider the inter-ests and concerns of other people and the community. These were traits instilled in me by my parents. I also give credit to my heri-tage. My Irish side helped me enjoy a level of comfort and humor in dealing with people and my Slovak side offered a thoughtful stoicism allowing me to contemplate issues at hand without too much anxiety.

The smart CEO knows what he doesn't know and he bolsters his team by getting the skills he is missing through the people around him who are willing to be a part of the effort and provide support - whether it's financial acumen, technology capability, marketing skills, leadership in the organization or getting peo-ple to play together. It's a rare CEO who has all of the needed skills within him or herself and can simply lead the orchestra. Most everyone's got blind spots when it comes to abilities. The problem with a lot of CEOs is that they don't know they've got blind spots - or they don't care. Or, worse, they know it but won't admit it.

I have my blind spots, of course. One is misplaced trust. I have too often over-relied on people I thought were supportive, believ-ing they were part of the team and they weren't. In situations where I was unsuccessful it was usually because of people issues, not technology or financial or anything else. It was because of my misjudgment, my fault for not seeing the people-related problems. It's difficult sometimes for a CEO to see where people's strengths are and where they are supportive and where they aren't in the organization. I don't consider myself naïve, but like everyone else I have been fooled from time to time by a smart, smooth talker who feigned enthusiasm.

Being a CEO can be a lonely job, because people tell you what they think you want to hear. You've got to have the sensitivity, or enough people within the organization who you can rely on to tell you what's really going on. The reason I was successful with LCI was that I had a team of people who made me successful. There's no question in my mind about that. It was both skills and learned experience that helped me to make the decisions that I had to make to guide that ship. But we pulled together as a team, all in the same direction. Again, it's knowing what you know, knowing what you don't know, building around you people who are creative, supportive, and want to be a part of your effort. And that's what I did and why LCI was successful. My colleague at MCI, Jerry Taylor, once said to me: "If you want to be a leader, find a good parade and get out in front of it." That's excellent advice.

Being a CEO can be a paradoxical job. Quite often, you've got to be *quick* to move but *slow* to move at the same time. The quick-to-move part has to do with the adage about your first impression often being the right one. Some people call it gut instinct which is usually built from experience. Once you get a feeling that some-one's not functioning well on the job too often we procrastinate in changing the situation because of the disruptions it causes. I think it's important to move more quickly on these kinds of things. If you talk to most CEOs about their biggest mistakes, it's usually that they did not fire somebody that they should have or moved more quickly to get that person the training that they were missing if lack of skills was the issue. When it comes to solving other prob-lems, like changing an organizational structure that's not working, however, you want to move slowly on taking action until you've done all of your intelligence gathering. Very often, people come into your office and say: "Oh my God, this thing is blowing up over here or, you know, the bomb's about to go off." You don't want to react immediately; you want to act wisely. You've got to be very thoughtful about it. People have often said to me: "Geez, how can you be in the midst of this maelstrom and still maintain a sense of balance?" That's just my style. That's my nature. (It's one of my red thread strands.) It goes back to taking bombs and mines apart. If you panicked or were impulsive, you could die. You had to have as much information as possible before you took action. Do you clip the red wire or the blue wire? You had to be slow and fast at the same time. You had to be thoughtful yet decisive. One takes time; the other goes quickly, so it's a paradox.

The other paradox is that you have to be *loose* and *tight* at the same time. For example, if you're going to delegate authority and responsibility, then your information systems better be top notch. You want to give people authority to make decisions, but you better know what's going on in the company. If the ship starts to sink, you've got to know the ship is sinking. You want to be loose in allowing people to do their jobs but tight in the sense that you have to keep your metering systems in place.

The last paradox is that of *lead* and *lag* and I consider myself a student of this practice. When you take a medication, you want it to work right away, but sometimes it takes several days of building up before it works. In business, you've got to understand how long a process takes. For instance, if you're selling to a small company it takes a month or two before they can make a decision on it. If you're selling to big companies, it takes a longer time. You have to know how long a process usually takes before deciding to change your sales program. It's got to be understood in the planning process and the budgeting process by the company, the unit, division or the department head that a plan takes time to work. That doesn't obviate the need for people expressing disapproval with you if you're not getting there or if you're not making the headway that they think you should. At the same time, you have to let things work. Sometimes, you have to sit back and watch a process unfold. It's not always easy especially when everyone around you is anxious about the company's slow progress. One of the most obvious examples of understanding the importance of timing lags is the dilemma of dealing with governments. For example, the recent stimulus packages in the federal government to deal with the United States' deep recession have taken about four years to put into action as all the regulations and decisions at every level have become cumbersome. Understanding how long processes take and managing people's expectations is crucial to any leader's success.

I'm grateful for my success, and at this point in my life, I'm trying to give back. One way I'm doing this mostly is by serving on company boards as well as those of schools and other institutions. Currently I serve on five corporate boards. I have served in many capacities but currently mainly on the compensation and governance committees because I believe I can do the most good in these areas. In all cases, I try to bring a sense of balance and perspective and a longer view. My experience running successful companies as well as my reputation as a strategist, especially at McKinsey, is what I think has prompted board members to ask me to join. Of course, friendships play a role in some cases, but it's because they know me and trust me and understand the skills and experience that I bring. In other cases, boards found me through headhunters only through my reputation.

I have seen the position of CEO change in my lifetime. When I was in business school, the CEO of a company played a very respected role. He (there were few female CEOs of public companies then) was a leader and it was something you strived toward by staying within the company, working and hopefully getting it right. It took perseverance. Now, there's more mobility, a lot more of getting ahead in business by changing companies. Managers can't manage in every industry without being steeped in that industry. I find that most people are not willing to give the time it takes to become completely immersed in an industry so they can understand it fully enough to manage successfully.

Also, sadly, I see more people loyal to the balance sheet and the shareholder than to the community and, most importantly, to employees. Another change I've seen is in mergers and acquisitions where companies want to sell out to other companies so the largest investors can cash out. In too many cases, I see people building companies with the sole intent of selling them quickly rather than building an entity that lasts and is worthwhile to society.

When I look back at my career, I have some regrets as we all do, but I think the only thing that I truly lament is not being more balanced in my earlier life with my career and family. In many cases, I was an absentee dad. I was on the road an awful lot, leaving Sunday night and coming back Saturday morning. In today's business environment, we're blessed with communications technology that can keep us in touch with our families when we're away from home.

To me, this is the most important aspect of being a successful CEO: maintaining balance *and* surrounding yourself with people who can help you to succeed. In turn, you do what you can to help them realize their dreams. Being a CEO is not simply about beating out the other guy or the other company although we are all competitive. It's about working with others to achieve a common goal. To be successful, make others successful. There is nothing more rewarding than to look into people's eyes and together realizing that they are succeeding in accomplishing something that they probably never dreamed they could. To me, that's the ultimate success in business. This simple idea is lost on some leaders, but successful CEOs know this to be true.

Successful CEOs also know that they have a red thread - the traits that follow them through their careers. For me, the red thread strands weren't always obvious at the time but have become clear with the passage of time. By taking risks, displaying balance, strong ethics, loyalty, self-discipline, helping people (and allowing them to help me), and taking a long view, I have been able to succeed in my business and personal life.

Index

Praise for *The Red Thread*

"One of the most difficult challenges any business leader faces is finding those people who are oriented to do the right thing, get the job done correctly and who enjoy solving problems. Brian believes in the importance of open and direct communication with the people in an organization, empowering managers to take chances and make decisions, and continually working to eliminate layers of bureaucracy."
— Roger S. Penske, Chairman, Penske Corporation

"Read this book. Learn from Brian's experience at less personal cost than he has paid. His candor and insights are reflected in the colorful fabric of his remarkable career."
— Vint Cerf, Internet pioneer

"Brian Thompson, a pioneer of the market based telecomm revolution, shares new insights and enduring wisdom about succeeding in business and in life. Must reading for aspiring entrepreneurs by a world class leader."
— Richard E. Cavanagh, Former CEO, the Conference Board Inc.; Former Executive Dean, Harvard Kennedy School

"Brian's leadership and mentoring became a life changing experience for me post my ABA/NBA career. I definitely learned from him what I missed by not attending graduate school. Additionally, I gained a friend and golfing buddy for life. What a blessing."
— Julius Erving, retired NBA and ABA player; former LCI board member

"*The Red Thread* is compelling and cogent. Brian unravels the fascinating world of telecommunications with straightforward clarity. It also is wonderful that he has helped put telecom and Ireland on the same page."
— Donald R. Keough, Chairman, Allen & Company; Former President of The Coca-Cola Company

For more information go to: www.the-red-thread-book.com

About the Author

*T*he *Red Thread* is a business memoir of H. Brian Thompson, one of the world's most successful telecommunications leaders, whose tenure has spanned from the start of the U.S.'s competitive telephone industry to today's internet connected world. A former Chairman of Comsat International, Thompson served as Chairman and CEO of LCI International, Inc., Non-Executive Chairman of Telecom Eireann, the Irish Telephone Company, Vice Chairman of Qwest and Executive Vice President of MCI Communications Corporation. In addition to serving on several boards of directors, he is a Former Chairman of CompTel, Co-Chairman of the Global Information Infrastructure Commission and a member of the Irish Prime Minister's Ireland-America Economic Advisory Board. Currently, he is Executive Chairman of GTT, the premier cloud network provider to the world.

Made in the USA
Middletown, DE
22 February 2018